D1098392

THE CLYDE AT WAR

THE CLYDE AT WAR

BRIAN D. OSBORNE
AND
RONALD ARMSTRONG

BIRLINN

This edition first published in 2005 by
Birlinn Limited
West Newington House
10 Newington Road
Edinburgh
EH9 1QS

Text copyright © 2001 Brian D. Osborne and Ronald Armstrong
Illustration credits appear on p. 6

The right of Brian D. Osborne and Ronald Armstrong to be identified as the authors
of this work has been asserted by them in accordance with the Copyright,
Designs and Patents Act 1988.

All rights reserved.
No part of this publication may be reproduced, stored, or transmitted in any form, or by
any means, electronic, mechanical or photocopying, or recording or otherwise, without the
express written permission of the publisher.

ISBN 1 84341 018 4

British Library cataloguing-in-Publication Data
A catalogue record for this book is available from the British Library

Text design by Jim hutcheson
Typeset by Patty Rennie Production, Glenbervie

Printed and bound by The Bath Press, Bath

CONTENTS

ILLUSTRATION CREDITS

Glasgow University Archive Plates 2, 37, 52, 53, 60, 61, 88, 89

James Hall 3, 4, 5, 6, 8, 9, 10, 11, 12, 13, 14, 15, 17, 18, 19, 20, 21, 22, 38, 39, 40, 41, 42, 43, 46, 47, 48, 54, 68, 69, 70, 71, 72, 73, 74, 75, 76, 77, 78, 79, 103, 104, 111, 112, 113, 114, 115

Glasgow City Libraries 7

Imperial War Museum 16, 36, 44, 45, 49, 50, 55, 59, 62, 63, 64, 65, 80, 81, 82, 92, 93, 94, 95, 100, 105, 107, 108, 109, 110

Tom Wilson 23, 24, 25, 26, 27, 28, 29, 30, 31, 32, 33, 34, 35

US Sources 56, 57, 58

West Dunbartonshire Libraries 66, 85, 87, 102, 116

Jim Adie 67

Argyll and Bute Libraries 83

East Dunbartonshire Libraries 84, 86, 90, 91, 96, 97, 98, 99, 101

Miscellaneous 106

Muirhead Bone 51

The Scottish Field 106

Special thanks are due to the following for their interest and support and for permission to use their recollections and photographs:

Tom Wilson

Jim Adie

Many thanks also to John and Norman Macphail for permission to quote extensively from their late father, the distinguished and most clubbable of historians and teachers, Dr I.M.M. Macphail.

CHAPTER 1

Introduction:
The Clyde at war through history

We fought; he fell beneath my sword. The banks of Clutha heard his fall; a thousand spears glittered around.

James Macpherson, *Carthon*

Plate 1
Dumbarton Rock as drawn by John Slezer.

The strategic significance in wartime of the River Clyde, its firth and sea lochs and adjacent islands, has been apparent since earliest times. Its significance is a result of the shelter afforded for all sorts of vessels by this vast natural harbour on the west coast of Scotland, its convenience for sea routes to Ireland, to other parts of the British Isles and beyond, and its proximity to inland power bases and (later) large centres of population. At the same time – in military and political terms – the position of the Clyde basin meant that it lay open to aggressive movements, not only from the north and west, as in the case of Norse invaders, but also from the emerging Scottish kingdom in the south and east. Later, the Stewart kings of Scotland dispatched expeditions from the River Clyde against unruly islanders. Then, in the twentieth century, particularly in the second of two world wars and in a period which included the Cold War, the river assumed a global significance.

That from earliest times the Clyde, or *Clutha*, was a river of strategic military importance can be inferred from the period of Roman occupation. The Antonine Wall could be outflanked from the river at its westernmost point at what we now call Old Kilpatrick – hence the Romans taking steps to erect watchtowers on the south bank near Greenock. Probably the most crucial and commanding feature of the river before it opens into the firth is Dumbarton Rock or *Alcluith*: the Rock on the Clyde. It is reasonable to suppose that the Rock was taken into the Roman sphere of influence, even if the hoax about it being a naval base named *Theodosia* can be discounted. Certainly in the centuries following the Roman departure, *Alcluith*, under the Britons of Strathclyde, played an important role in Dark Age politics and presumably in wars too, since politics and war were virtually synonymous.

The Britons of Strathclyde are believed to have commanded a territory which at its peak extended from the head of Loch Lomond to at least Morecambe Bay. Their language was probably akin to Welsh; certainly most of the information we have about this shadowy people comes from Welsh sources. It can be presumed that there was at one time some seaborne navigation from Wales to the Clyde and its wider firth (The Cumbraes, islands in the Firth, bear a Welsh name from the same root as *Cymry*, meaning 'the Welsh'). The Clyde probably also marked some kind of frontier with the Gaelic-speaking kingdom of the Scots to the north in Argyll, and there may have been tension between the two.

The First World War in the Clyde

A K-class submarine is seen in the River Clyde in **plate 2**. *Note the twin funnels behind the conning tower, which have to be covered when the vessel submerges. This is a sister-ship of K13, which was tragically lost in the Gareloch in 1915. Just after noon on 19 January 1917, HMS K13, on trials in the Gareloch, signalled to nearby HMS E50 her intention to dive. As the submarine submerged the engine room began to flood. The submarine became uncontrollable and came to rest on the bottom with the engine room and after torpedo room flooded. The crew of E50, witnessing K13's rapid dive, closed in on the area, discovering traces of oil and escaping air breaking the surface. The first rescue vessel arrived around midnight. Divers were sent down to inspect the submarine and just after daybreak on 20 January morse signals were exchanged between the divers and the trapped crew. At 17.00 an air-line was successfully connected, empty air bottles recharged and ballast tanks blown. With the aid of a hawser slung under her bows K13 was brought to within 8 feet of the surface. By midday on 21 January K13's bow had been raised 10 feet above the water. By 21.00 the pressure hull had been breached using oxyacetylene cutting equipment and the survivors transferred to safety. K13 was finally raised on 15 March, refitted and returned to service as HMS K22. Thirty-one dead are buried in Faslane Cemetery.*

Plate 2

It is certain that when the latest key force in Scotland's power politics came along in the shape of the Vikings, the Clyde was to figure in a number of campaigns which saw Norse (and later Scoto-Norse) invaders encroaching on the British kingdom. Raids were launched on the Rock of the Clyde, notably in 870 AD and again in 1164 by Somerled, the half-Scots, half-Norse sub-king of Argyll. He took a force of 160 galleys upriver to Renfrew intent on subduing 'all Scotland to himself'. The *Chronicle of Melrose* reported on this early instance of the Clyde at war:

> Somerled, the regulus of Argyle, wickedly rebelling for now twelve years against Malcolm, the King of Scots, his natural lord, after he had landed at Renfrew, bringing a large army from Ireland and various places, was at last through divine vengeance slain there…

Somerled's head was then taken to Glasgow to be exhibited before its bishop. The King of Scots in question was one of those who reigned following the union of the Picts and Scots; the Britons of Strathclyde had also joined the united kingdom by the time that the Norse played their last card. In 1263 Haakon IV of Norway ravaged the west in a bid to retain hegemony over the whole seaboard – one raiding party sailed up Loch Long, dragged their ships overland to Tarbet and sailed down Loch Lomond to plunder the Lennox.

There are also very many islands in that lake, and well-inhabited. The Norwegians wasted these islands with fire. They burned also all the dwellings all around the lake.

Frisbok's Hakon Hakon's Son's Saga

However this was to be the last successful intrusion of the dreaded 'fury' of the Norsemen into the Clyde basin. Later the same year Hakon and the major part of his invasion fleet were lying at anchor further down the Firth of Clyde at Largs. Some ships were driven onshore by strong winds and their crews forced into battle with a sizeable Scottish army. Short of supplies and far from their base, the Norwegian force withdrew. Although not a major clash of arms, Largs proved a turning point, as the last episode of extensive Norse intervention throughout mainland Scotland.

Plates 3 and 4 (opposite)

Largs also signalled a time when the Clyde featured less in national politics and in naval and military strategy. To a great extent the emphasis shifted to the Central Scotland and the East Coast, although admittedly both William Wallace and King Robert the Bruce had strong connections with the west – Wallace with Elderslie and Bruce with Arran, the Carrick shore, and several other places in the area – according to legend at any rate.

It is certain that Robert I spent his last years at Dumbarton and the Lord Treasurer's Accounts mention a 'Great Ship' in the River Leven above where it flows into the Clyde. This may be evidence that the Scottish monarchy maintained a naval presence in the west and a first recorded example of shipbuilding capability.

As has been mentioned, the later Stewart kings did use the Clyde, and in particular Dumbarton with its royal castle at the place 'where two rivers meet', as a strategic base to launch 'expeditions' to the Highlands and Islands, usually with some kind of pacifying intent, or in the phrase used at the time, for 'the daunting of the Isles'. James IV and James V took part in such expeditions themselves while building a sizeable navy, taking advantage of the woodlands of Loch Lomondside to provide timber for shipbuilding. One of the final chapters of Queen Mary's reign was enacted near the Clyde at the Battle of Langside in 1568, while James VI campaigned in and around Kintyre with the same intentions as his predecessors.

The boom defence on the Clyde

In both world wars a boom defence system was installed across the river to protect the great natural anchorage of the Tail of the Bank and the adjacent sea lochs from intruding submarines. The protected anchorage thus created was put to good use, especially in the Second World War as the dramatic scene in **plate 3** *clearly shows. The First World War image of the boom (* **plate 4** *) is taken*

The "Cloch" lighthouse, from Dunoon. "Clyde"

from Dunoon (the statue of Burns' 'Highland Mary' can be seen in the foreground) looking across the line of floats and nets to the Cloch Lighthouse near Gourock. That the submarine threat in a supposedly defended harbour was no idle one was proved by the loss, in 1939, of the battleship HMS Royal Oak at Scapa Flow. After the sinking of the Royal Oak elements of the Home Fleet used the Clyde as an anchorage, despite the strategic disadvantage of its distance from the North Sea theatre of operations. The difficulties of penetrating the Clyde were perhaps greater and only one attempt seems to have been made – U33, commanded by Kapitänleutnant Hans-Wilhelm von Dresky, was sunk on 12 February 1940 in the Clyde estuary, about five miles south of Pladda, while on a minelaying mission. She was detected by the minesweeper HMS Gleaner using hydrophones and repeatedly attacked with depth-charges. She surfaced and the conning tower crew surrendered but her captain and some twenty of her crew were killed as the submarine's scuttling charges exploded. The German naval commander-in-chief, Admiral Raeder, advised Hitler, who had ordered the mission, that such an enterprise was too risky and would not be repeated. The dead from U33 were buried in Greenock, and **plate 5**, *taken in March 1946, shows a group of German POWs, then working on building sites in Greenock, who had obtained permission to hold a memorial service for the crew. The loss of the U33 was of considerable significance to the Allied war effort as three rotors for the 'Enigma' cipher machine were recovered from the survivors – thus assisting the cryptographers at Bletchley Park in the task breaking of the German naval codes and helping to overcome the threat to convoys from the U-boat menace. The boom defence remained operational however and* **plate 6**, *taken from the Renfrewshire coast with the Cloch Lighthouse in the foreground, gives an excellent impression of the complex nature of the system and the number of ships that were needed to operate it and pass*

Plate 5

vessels through the boom. Commercial steamer sailings were firmly divided between routes above and below the boom.

Plate 6

In the Gaelic-speaking area of the Clyde Basin the warlike qualities of the chiefs and their followers were still celebrated in bardic song. Here is the Bard of the MacEwens in praise of the seventeenth chief of Clan Campbell, Gillesbeg Gruamach, Marquis of Argyll:

> He is a veteran to defend our bounds, he is our diadem of gold, our abiding mansion; his hand is like Oscar's in hour of action, he is our sheltering vine. Whether others be at peace or at war, MacCailin is our firm defence; his hand is followed as a wave of fruitfulness; he is the Hector of the land of Scotland . . . without peer in feats of battle.

The Clyde next entered a phase when it was to become more celebrated for flourishing trade and industry than as a setting for warfare, apart, that is, from the irruption of Charles Edward Stuart's Highland army into Glasgow in 1746. The great days of sail and the men o' war were centred more on the Channel and North Sea ports, although enemies began to see that Britain, as an island, could be blockaded from the sea – witness incidents like the raids on British shipping led by the renegade Kirkcudbright man and founder of the US Navy, John Paul Jones. American privateers also operated in and around Clyde waters during the war of 1812, as described by Walter Scott in a diary of his 1815 cruise in the Lighthouse Yacht *Pharos*:

> [Off the coast of Kintyre] We then learn that we have been repeatedly in the route of two American privateers, who have made many captures in the Irish Channel. Particularly at Innistruhul, at the back of Islay, and on the Lewis.

The rise of the city of Glasgow led to a new awareness of the Atlantic dimension, as did the growth of the tobacco and cotton trades. Glasgow's trading position soon outstripped other burghs in the west, such as Renfrew and Dumbarton. A shift of political emphasis from Europe to America and attendant wars saw these trades dwindle, but others took their place, and with the opening up of the river to navigation Glasgow entered the period of the Industrial Revolution as 'The Second City of the Empire'. Shipbuilding all along both banks boomed (and just as frequently bust) and made 'Clyde-built' an epithet recognised the world over. Steam navigation came to the Clyde in the form of Henry Bell's *Comet*. Bell offered it to the Admiralty in 1813, but steam warships were a technological development whose hour had not yet come. It arrived with the 'Father of Clyde Shipbuilding', Robert Napier, who built the iron steamers *Jackal*, *Lizard* and *Bloodhound* for the Royal Navy in the 1840s. Napier went on to build the navy's second ever 'ironclad', HMS *Black Prince*, which was among the first large warships not built in the Royal Naval Dockyards.

The Clyde took a hand in North American affairs once again when some of the river's fine steamers had careers as blockade-runners for the Confederate states during the Civil War. Steamers like the *Eagle* and the *Jupiter* were bought by undercover Confederate agents, desperate for fast ships to elude Union patrols. One, the *Iona*, was painted grey and stripped of her fine furnishings in the Clyde, but going downriver showing no lights she was run down and sunk by another vessel off Gourock.

Early casualties 1   Plate 7

The impact of hostilities in the Second World War was not long in coming to the Clyde. In the Atlantic, the U-boats were having greater success – a number of sinkings of neutral and British ships was followed by the sad sight of survivors appearing on the dockside at Greenock, having been picked up by Royal Navy ships. The first and probably most poignant of these was the torpedoing of the SS Athenia of the Donaldson Shipping Line on an Atlantic crossing to Montreal, in the first few hours following the declaration of war on 3 September. Many of the survivors, including US citizens, were taken to Glasgow and **plate 7** *shows some of the youngest meeting the Lord Provost of Glasgow, Pat Dollan, at the Central Hotel, on 7 September. Standing on the Lord Provost's left is the unmistakable figure of the young John Fitzgerald Kennedy, son of the American Ambassador in London and future President of the United States. Note the sandbags at the hotel entrance.*

In the twentieth century a number of companies on the Clyde specialised in warship building, albeit mostly in the war years themselves, since quality merchant shipbuilding still dominated the entries in the order books. Clydebank,

Fairfield's and Dalmuir made the most significant contribution to the Royal Navy in the First World War, but smaller yards like Denny's and Scott's each had their specialities, destroyers and submarines among them. Clyde-built naval shipping during the war amounted to 487 different vessels totalling almost a million tons. They included 159 destroyers, of which twenty-four came from Beardmore's yard. Clyde-built warships amounted to 40 per cent of all Admiralty orders in the fifty years up to the outbreak of the Second World War.

Plate 8 (opposite)

Plate 9 (overleaf)

The Clyde was one of the ports to and from which the vital convoys of supply-bearing merchant ships made their voyages. Munitions works produced millions of shells and 50 000 men and women were employed to make them – in some of them it was said that the prevailing language was not English but Gaelic. This was indicative of the pool of labour on which Glasgow could draw and of the strong Gaelic influence in the city. Engineering firms made everything from railway engines to tanks; by 1918, 90 per cent of all armour plate for British tanks was being produced on the Clyde.

'The Battle of the Atlantic' was a term coined during the Second World War by Winston Churchill but one which could have been equally appropriate to the 1914–18 war. In both major wars of the twentieth century the convoy system and the ultimate defeat of the German U-boats was absolutely pivotal to the outcome of the conflict. This was largely the result of strategies evolved with the Clyde in mind. Moreover, Clydeside with its engineering tradition made a major contribution to the provision of armaments for these global conflicts. In the First World War, for example, the people of Glasgow and the Clyde enlisted in proportionately greater numbers than other parts of Britain as they rushed to join the tartan-clad regiments, such as the Highland Light Infantry (HLI), the Royal Scots Fusiliers and the Argyll and Sutherland Highlanders. The Second World War introduced a new element, a new front – now for the first time in hundreds of years war was brought home directly to Clydesiders, but in a novel way: war from the air in the form of the blitz.

Early casualties 2

The City of Benares *was built on the Clyde and launched from Barclay, Curle's yard, in August 1936. The flagship of the Ellerman Line, her pre-war service was on the route between Liverpool and Bombay. In September 1940 she was sailing to Canada with several hundred children on board, evacuees being sent for safety to homes in North America. Six hundred miles out she was torpedoed by U48 and quickly sank.* **Plate 8** *shows one of the ship's boats with half a dozen children and a number of the* City of Benares *Lascar crew and an officer at the helm. Like many British shipping lines trading to India, Ellerman's deck crew was traditionally recruited from the sub-continent.* **Plate 9** *shows five of the youthful survivors of the tragedy. In all 248 people, including seventy-seven children, lost their lives on the* City of Benares. *The boat seen in plate 8 was spotted by an RAF*

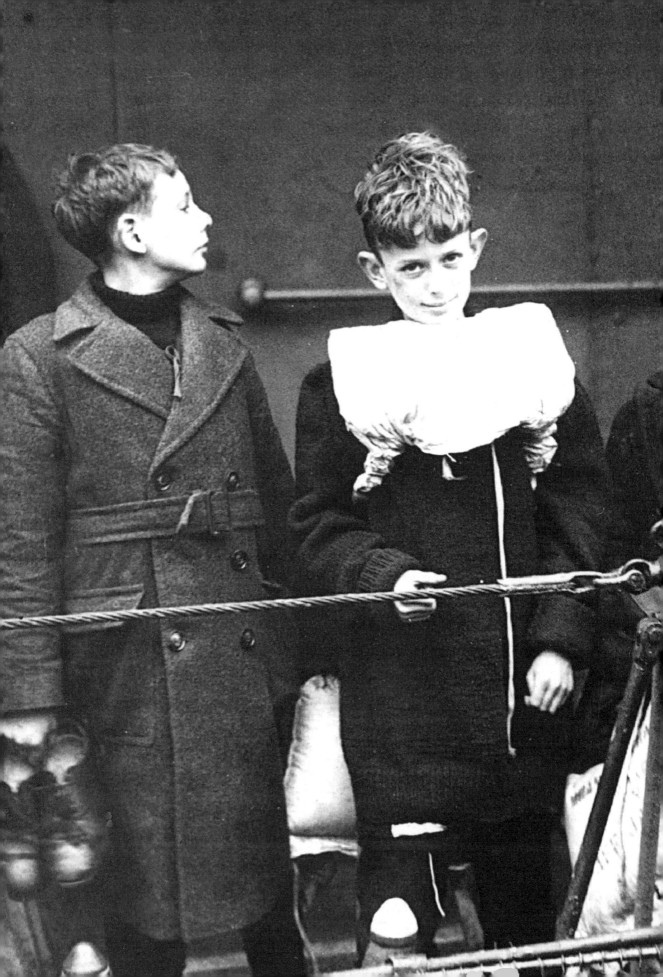

Plate 10

Coastal Command Sunderland flying-boat which despatched the destroyer Anthony *to rescue it. The* Anthony *was built by Scotts at Greenock in 1927.* **Plate 10** *shows a boy from the* City of Benares *(clearly the second on the left in the previous plate) on the shoulders of a sailor. It will be seen that the ship's name on the sailor's cap-tally has been obliterated in the plate at the instructions of the censor; however the name can be deciphered and is HMS* Anthony. **Plate 11** *shows a very young survivor, the three-month-old Jessie Hunt, in the arms of a sailor from the destroyer HMS* Hurricane, *which was one of the first ships on the scene. Oddly enough the cap-ribbon has escaped the censor's watchful eye – possibly this picture was not published at the time.*

Glasgow and the Clyde also had, it turned out, a very important role to play in the involvement of the (still neutral) United States in the Second World War. This hinged upon a visit to Scotland in 1941 made by President Roosevelt's greatly trusted special envoy, Harry Hopkins, at the invitation of Prime Minister Churchill. At the time the US President was under great pressure not to engage his country in the war and not to give any commitments which might lead to any position other than strict neutrality. Hopkins and Churchill came to Glasgow and were welcomed by Tom Johnston, the Regional Commissioner (and soon to be Secretary of State) for Scotland. The latter wrote in his book *Memories* that Hopkins was giving nothing away regarding any commitments –

he was, Johnston wrote, 'poker faced and dumb as an oyster'. At a dinner held in the North British Station Hotel, beside George Square, Johnston was in the chair and made an attempt to draw the presidential 'confidential agent' out, as he described in this extract from *Memories*:

> During the dinner I had discovered from Harry Hopkins that his grand-mother or his great-grandmother had been born at Auchterarder in Perthshire . . .
>
> 'We have tonight,' I said, 'with us a friend from overseas. If he cares to say a word to us, we shall all be delighted. This is quite an informal gathering; no press representative is present. And more particularly do I welcome Mr Hopkins for the sake of his old grandmother from Auchterarder.'

Hopkins' emotional reply, Johnston recalled, ran something like the following:

Plate 11

> Mr Chairman, I am not making speeches over here. I am reporting what I see to Mr Franklin Delano Roosevelt, my President, a great man, a very great man. But now I am here and on my feet perhaps I might say in the language of the old book to which my grandmother from Auchterarder, and no doubt your grandmother too, Mr Chairman, paid so much attention, that, [and here Hopkins paused and looked straight down the table at Churchill] 'Wheresoever thou goest we go, and where thou lodgest we lodge, thy people shall be our people, thy God our God, even to the end.'

And following this quotation from the Book of Ruth, he sat down. Johnston concluded: 'Here was the first news that the United States was throwing its weight upon the Allied side.'

Disaster

The French destroyer Maillé-Brézé *had had a busy spring in 1940. She had crossed the Atlantic escorting the battleship* Bretagne *and the cruiser* Algérie *which were carrying French gold reserves to safety in Canada. In early April she had gone to combat the German naval forces invading Norway and in mid-April had escorted French troops (the 5me Demi-Brigade of the Chasseurs D'Alpin) to Namsos. By 30 April she was at Greenock for maintenance and her crew were shifting torpedoes when one accidentally exploded. The destroyer swiftly sank and twenty-eight of the crew were killed. Seven were buried in Greenock Cemetery but the bodies of the remainder were in a compartment that could not be reached before the ship sank. These three photographs were taken in 1954 when the Admiralty salvaged the* Maillé-Brézé. *She was moved from where she lay to the Ardmore sandbank and the remaining munitions on board were removed, including eighteen depth-charges. The remains of the twenty-one of her crew who had not been recovered in 1940 were taken*

Plate 12 (previous page)

Plate 13 (opposite)

Plate 14 (above)

ashore in August 1954 with full naval honours and Requiem Mass was held in St Laurence's Church, Greenock, before the remains were returned to France for burial. The wreck was then taken to the Port Glasgow breaker's yard of Smith and Houston and broken up in October 1954. **Plate 12** *shows the ship newly raised from the Clyde and gives a good impression of this large (2441 tons displacement) and powerful destroyer, which was launched at St Nazaire in 1930 and entered service in 1933. The two forward 5.5-inch guns are well seen in this image. In addition to her main*

Plate 15 (previous page)

armament of five 5.5-inch guns the ship – classed as a contre-torpilleur *– also mounted seven torpedo tubes. She was named after a seventeenth-century Grand Admiral of France.* **Plate 13** *is a general view on the main deck looking from the stern while scrapping operations are under way.* **Plate 14** *shows the area where the torpedo exploded.*

Later in the conflict, when the Americans had formally joined the Allies and Roosevelt and Churchill were planning the strategy of global war, the Clyde area was thrust into the frontline again. This was in the build-up to the invasion of North Africa, when most of the invasion fleet for Operation Torch was assembled in the river. Yet again, the Clyde was a vital staging post for the ultimate invasion of Normandy, when it became the most important reception port for hundreds of thousands of American GIs and other Allied troops, as one pillar of an 'Atlantic Bridge'. In parallel with the shipping in of personnel, there was a top-secret mass movement of hundreds of aircraft from North America via Iceland and Greenland into Prestwick Airport.

The grey giant

*In this most evocative photograph (***plate 15***) the giant Cunard liner* Queen Elizabeth, *in wartime grey, is pictured leaving John Brown's shipyard in Clydebank on 25 January 1940 before setting out on her unescorted dash (and first-ever trip) across the Atlantic to New York. The war career of the* Queen Elizabeth *and her elder sister-ship* Queen Mary *was to be extremely exciting and vital to Britain's war effort.*

Most of the plates and background material in this book reflect the overwhelming impact of the two great wars of the twentieth century. However, it will be noted that the Clyde remains in the forefront of strategic defence thinking in the post-war period because of the siting of nuclear missile submarines, by the US at the Holy Loch during much of the Cold War period, and by the UK right up to the present day at Faslane. HM Naval Base Clyde, as at March 2001, hosts HQ Flag Officer Scotland, Northern England and Northern Ireland (FOSNNI). In addition to housing the four Vanguard-class Trident ballistic missile submarines and five Superb-class nuclear powered hunter-killer submarines of the 1st Submarine Squadron, the Faslane base provides sea training for the crews of all Royal Navy submarines.

As a footnote: the mention of Faslane reminds us that if the Clyde is known for war, so it is also known for peace; the twentieth century and now the twenty-first has a long list of people known for their forcible expression – in the Clydesider's usual fashion – of pacifist opinions.

CHAPTER 2

War at sea

I've helped to build a wheen o' them in mony a different yaird,
Frae barges up to battleships the Empire for to guaird,
An' eh, the names I could reca' o' men noo passed awa'
Wha planned and built the boats lang syne, aye trig and strang and braw.
The men hae gane, but left ahint a legacy o' fame,
For honest wark an' bonny boats that gied the Clyde its name.

J.F. Fergus, *The Yairds*

Plate 16

Destroyers and a cruiser steaming in line towards port in Firth of Clyde. Arran and the Holy Isle are in the background.

The twentieth century involved the River Clyde heavily in naval wars with a completely new global dimension. This was because the Atlantic, and beyond that the other oceans of the world, was now a sphere in which British naval strategy operated just as much as the North Sea, the Mediterranean or the Channel. The twentieth century also brought great changes in naval tactics and techniques. Previously it was thought that naval warfare would continue in the classic pattern of ships-of-the-line delivering massive broadsides, but the invention of the ironclads and Dreadnoughts with their huge turret-mounted guns delivering massive high-explosive shells over great distances took it in quite a different direction.

Even before the entry of the USA and the need to keep open her vital lines of communication, western ports like the Clyde with direct access to the Atlantic played an increasingly important role and held the key to Britain's supply routes. In the Second World War German occupation of most of the Continent meant they controlled the coasts from the Baltic to the Bay of Biscay and Allied commercial shipping had great difficulty in entering many ports, including London itself. For a while, in the early months of the war, the Clyde was even made the base for the Home Fleet because of concerns about the security of Scapa Flow. Prime Minister Winston Churchill, writing in *The Second World War* in 1950, described the situation regarding Britain's trading position in 1941:

The ports themselves, particularly those on the East Coast, were subject to attack which might temporarily paralyse them. London, by far our

| **31**

main port, was largely immobilised owing to the risk of sending large vessels round to the East Coast in the face of attacks by air, by E-boats and by mines. Thus the East Coast ports could not take their full share of the load, and the greater burden fell upon the ports in the west – Liverpool, the Clyde and the Bristol Channel.

Germany's naval strategy in both wars of the twentieth century sought to mount a blockade of British shipping. On both occasions the German plan almost succeeded – twice in half a century the Western Approaches to the British Isles became a hunting ground for German raiders (submarines and large surface ships like the *Emden* in the First World War, and the *Admiral Scheer* in the Second) and vital supply-lines were throttled and close to being cut altogether. Food shortages of every kind resulted from the Germans' sinking of over 2600 ships by the end of 1917, a total of 11 million tons of shipping. A quarter of a century on and there was a period when London and all Atlantic ports were blockaded by mines or intensive bombing but principally by the U-boat menace – even Liverpool was rendered inoperative by bombing. The Clyde alone remained open to the ships and supplies which did manage to get past the undersea raiders – a vital sea artery which continued to pump life into Britain. It was a close shave, however. Even in late 1942 and early 1943 millions of tons of shipping were being sunk.

The Battle of the Atlantic

Clyde-bound convoys brought in many of the essential materials to continue the war. **Plate 17** *shows a ship carrying, as deck cargo, twin-engined bombers built in North American factories. It will be seen that the tail assemblies of the aircraft are not yet fitted – this enabled more aircraft to be loaded on board. Later, many larger planes from Canada and in due course the USA were ferried in directly by air to Prestwick – this was known as the 'Atlantic bridge'.* **Plate 18** *shows merchant seamen on deck looking out over an Atlantic convoy. An escort vessel can be seen manoeuvering between the columns. The Merchant Navy sustained huge losses of men and ships – in the North Atlantic itself, British, Allied and neutral sinkings amounted to 496 vessels totalling 2 421 700 tons in 1941 alone. Enemy aircraft posed an obvious threat from bombs and cannon but also could guide waiting U-boats into the path of a convoy.* **Plate 19** *shows a naval gunner on duty at his 20-millimetre Oerlikon anti-aircraft gun. It will be noted that the censor has instructed details of the gun-sight to be obliterated. In* **plate 20** *the Royal Canadian Navy corvette* Hepatica *is seen making a wet crossing in defence of a Clyde-bound convoy. The tiny pre-war Canadian navy was vastly expanded to help win the Battle of the Atlantic. Much of its effort went into building and manning a new class of small, ocean-going anti-submarine escort vessels – the corvette. The* Hepatica *was one of an early group of Flower-class corvettes ordered from Canadian yards for the Royal Navy. She was however reassigned to the Canadian Navy when completed in November 1940. The censor has*

instructed that her pennant number, K159, painted on her bows, should be blocked out. Corvette

K120 HMS Borage *is shown off Gourock in* **plate 21**. Borage, *a Flower-class corvette, was built*

at George Brown and Company's Garvel Yard at Greenock and launched in November 1941. From

her smart and un-weatherbeaten appearance this photograph would seem to have been taken shortly

after her completion and acceptance trials. After war service as a convoy escort on the North

Atlantic Borage *was sold to the Irish Navy in 1946 and served there as the* Maev. *Note the anti-aircraft barrage balloon overhead and the minesweeping gear on deck at the stern of the* Borage. *Most corvettes were equipped to act as minesweepers as well as their primary role as anti-submarine vessels. In* **plate 22** *we see a Canadian sailor writing home, while sitting in the sunshine on a depth-charge on an escort corvette.*

What proved to be the decisive move in the Battle of the Atlantic, and one in which the Clyde also played a crucial role, was the wholehearted implementation of the convoy system and the introduction of technological changes that saved the merchant marine, and, through convoy escorts – at sea and in the air – provided a platform from which to launch a counter-attack against German raiders.

Plate 22

In earliest times a convoy meant a group of neutral vessels sailing together for mutual protection under the 'convoy' of warships also belonging to a neutral power. By the twentieth century convoys meant something completely different. They were a defensive device employed by one of the belligerent powers – in this case the UK and her Allies – against unrestricted German submarine warfare, which was also directed against neutral shipping, including that belonging to the USA. Large numbers of merchant ships (many of them crewed by merchant seamen from communities around the river), sailed to and from the Clyde, organised into convoys protected by as many escort vessels, such as destroyers, as could be spared from other duties. In 1942, for example, twenty-four destroyers and thirteen corvettes made up escort groups based on Greenock, covering not only North Atlantic convoys but Arctic convoys as well. Typically, the merchantmen would sail in columns in line astern with an outer screen of destroyers, and other smaller warships like corvettes (later frigates). Escorts armed with depth-charges and guns were usually more than a match for submarines, especially when the U-boats were operating on the surface, which they had to do a lot of the time. Devices such as radio, ASDIC and radar made a significant difference when they were introduced and perfected. In both wars, curiously, the wholehearted adoption of the convoy system only came after a period when losses of Allied merchant ships had reached unacceptable levels.

In **plate 23**, HMS *Archer is seen on flying trials in the Firth Of Clyde, with two Swordfish and one Gruman Martlet on deck. She was the first of the* Archer *class of twenty-three escort carriers and was given to Britain by the USA in 1942 as a stop-gap until further carriers could be built.* Archer *had been built at the Tacoma yards in Washington State in 1939, with a 14 500-ton displacement and a 450-foot flight deck on top of a merchant-ship hull. The 'Woolworth' carrier as she was known (because of the rapidity of the mass-production methods employed) crossed the Atlantic with a full complement of US servicemen bound for the European and North African battlefields. Under Royal Navy command and with the Clyde as her main port, she was next loaded with aircraft flown into Abbotsinch and took up a different, absolutely crucial role. This can best be described by an extract from newspapers in July 1943, written at the point when the Battle of the Atlantic was raging and transatlantic convoys were under severe U-boat attack in that part of the Atlantic crossing which could not be protected by land-based aircraft. The* Sunday Express *wrote: 'The Admiralty, releasing news last night of the smashing of U-boat nest in the Atlantic "gap" and the safe journey of a valuable convoy from America to Britain, provides new evidence that the U-boat menace in the Atlantic, upon which Hitler built his highest hopes, is being effectively countered. Under the new system the gap has been bridged by ship-based planes . . . For the first stages of the crossing close air-cover was provided by Hudson, Ventura, Liberator and Catalina aircraft of the Royal Canadian Air Force. When these reached the limit of their range the cover was taken over by Swordfish and Martlet aircraft from the escort carrier* Archer. *In a series of attacks that extended over two days one U-boat was destroyed, another was probably destroyed, and others may have been damaged. During the final stage of the passage air escort was provided by Liberators, Sunderlands and Halifaxes of Coastal Command . . . in future Allied convoys can cross the Atlantic freely with the assurance that they will be guarded all the way by aircraft either shore-based or carrier-borne.'*

Plate 23 (overleaf)

In the Second World War the importance of the role of Canada in protecting convoys with naval (and air) operations cannot be underestimated. The Royal Canadian Navy grew from a pre-war strength of only 1800 to almost 100 000 and most of its war effort went into the manning of corvettes and other escort vessels. Canadian yards built over 130 corvettes and by early 1943 almost half the escorts assigned to the main North Atlantic convoy routes were Canadian. The corvette, whether British or Canadian, was the workhorse of the Atlantic convoy: small, simple, lightly manned, manoeuvrable, cheap to construct, lightly armed with depth-charges, a four-inch gun and some anti-aircraft weapons. When the U-boats were creating mayhem on the eastern US seaboard and the Caribbean in 1942 (what Churchill called 'The U-boat Paradise'), corvettes were sent to assist the Americans, who were quite ill-equipped for anti-submarine warfare at that stage. The corvette design was later expanded and formed the origins of the frigate class of escort vessels. Technological aspects dominated what Churchill dubbed 'The Battle of the Atlantic':

Directive by the Minister of Defence, March 6, 1941

- In view of various German statements, we must assume that the Battle of the Atlantic has begun. The next four months should enable us to defeat the attempt to strangle our food supplies and our connection with the United States. For this purpose:

- We must take the offensive against the U-boat and the Focke–Wulf wherever we can. The U-boat at sea must be hunted, the U-boat in the building yard or in dock must be bombed. The Focke–Wulf and other bombers employed against our shipping must be attacked in the air and in their nests.

- Extreme priority will be given to fitting out ships to catapult or otherwise launch fighter aircraft against bombers attacking our shipping.

- All the measures approved and now in train for the concentration of the main strength of the Coastal Command upon the North-Western Approaches . . . will be pressed forward. It may be hoped that, with the growing daylight and the new routes to be followed, the U-boat menace will soon be reduced. All the more important is it that the Focke–Wulf, and, if it comes, the Junkers 88, should be effectively grappled with.

- We must be ready to meet concentrated air attacks on the ports on which we specially rely (Mersey, Clyde and Bristol Channel). They must therefore be provided with a maximum defence.

The advantage swung first of all the way of the Germans, when they introduced the tactic of deploying U-boats in 'wolf packs'. (The Focke–Wulf long-range bombers, about which the Minister was so concerned, did sink thirty ships in a matter of two months but fortunately for the British were never properly co-ordinated with the U-boats). The Clyde was the unhappy recipient of many of the pitiful survivors of the torpedo attacks – from those picked up from the *Athenia*, which was struck a fatal blow just hours after the declaration of war, to the *Empress of Britain* and the *Lancastria*, and many more.

Flying from a carrier

The next sequence of **plates (24–26)** *shows the Swordfish fighter-bombers and the US-built Martlet fighters on Archer's flight deck. It will be evident just how dangerous a business this was – like 'landing on a plank'. Plates showing 'prangs' or crashes are evidence of this. Deck aircraft arrester gear and other items of equipment can be seen, together with the brave and skilled deck crew. HMS* Patroller *was a sister-ship of* Archer, *and here she is seen in bow view in the floating dock at Faslane Naval Base (***plate 27***). Her island bridge stands out against the background of the River Clyde (***plate 28***).*

Plate 24 (above)

Plate 25 (left)

Plate 26 (bellow)

The prototype of the Fairey Swordfish first flew as long ago as 1934 and it was considered to be on the verge of obsolescence at the outbreak of war in 1939. Despite this, the Swordfish went on to become one of the most versatile of the Second World War aircraft, and had among its battle honours the crippling of the Italian fleet at Taranto, the trapping and sinking of the Bismarck, and the breaking of the siege of Malta. Designed originally as a carrier-borne torpedo-bomber with spotter and reconnaissance capabilities, it played a vital part in the Battle of the Atlantic, as in the examples shown here. One of the last biplanes in service, the Swordfish in seaplane version had a maximum speed (incredibly) of only 128 m.p.h., but proved ideal for take-off and landing from the deck of an escort carrier in mid-ocean. In **plate 29** *the torpedo has been launched.*

Plate 27 (previous page)

Plate 28 (opposite)

Plate 29 (following page)

The German submarine warriors strove throughout to bring Britain to its knees. In February 1940 the U33 had been scuttled off Arran after entering the firth – on the direct orders of Hitler, it is said. The minesweeper HMS *Gleaner* picked her up on the hydrophone and launched a depth-charge attack. No submarine ever penetrated the Clyde's defences again. Out in the ocean, however, things went from bad to worse. Churchill wrote:

> Amid the torrent of violent events one anxiety reigned supreme. Battles might be won or lost, enterprises might succeed or miscarry, territories might be gained or quitted, but dominating all our power to carry on the war, or even keep ourselves alive, lay our mastery of the ocean routes and the free approach and entry to our ports. I have described . . . the perils that the German occupation of the coast of Europe from the North Cape to the Pyrenees brought upon us. From any port or inlet along this enormous front the hostile U-boats, constantly improving in speed, endurance, and radius, could sally forth to destroy our sea-borne food and trade.

In March 1943, just as in April 1917, the submarine offensive was on the brink of inflicting decisive damage on Britain's supply routes – 627377 tons of shipping sunk in that month alone. To use a Churchillian phrase, the tide turned when, amongst other things, a new Western Approaches Command was formed: this brought about for the first time effective co-operation between the RAF and the Royal Navy. Now the convoys were escorted by warships that could really be described as 'sub-killers' or by aircraft carriers – at first converted merchant ships doubling as escort aircraft carriers (such as HMS *Archer*); air support from carriers and merchant carriers was supplemented by long-range Liberator aircraft from airfields like Prestwick; and Allied technical innovations included improved short-wave radar detection and radio communications from bases such as the top-secret 'Signal City' (probably at a modest villa called 'Marymount', high above Gourock pier).

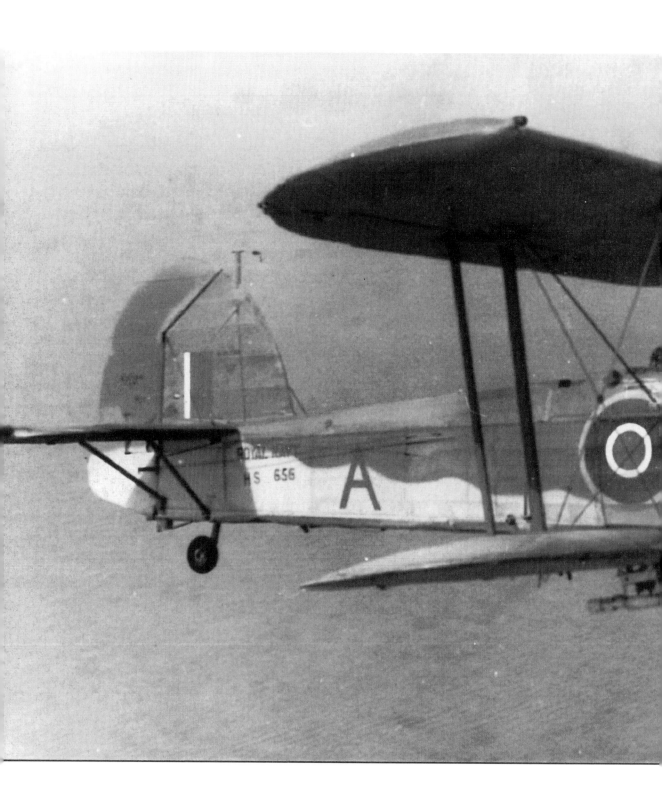

The build-up of Allied measures against U-boats was inexorable. Even when the latter were replaced by a new generation of vessels able to remain submerged for long periods – due to the invention of the 'schnorkel' or breathing tube – and with greater underwater speed and endurance, sinkings of Allied ships were still two-thirds less than they had been previously. The Battle of the Atlantic was well on the way to being won and the Allies had sufficient control of the sea to make the decisive move against the enemy in the Normandy landings of 1944.

Plate 30 (previous page)

An officer's life at sea

These two photographs show a more relaxed side of life on board Archer. *As a converted US merchant ship, she came with a far better quality of fittings and equipment for the use of the officers and crew than Royal Navy personnel were used to – the ship boasted a soda fountain, as can be seen in the photograph of the visit of* HM the King (**plate 30**). *The officers' wardroom* (**plate 31**) *shows some of the officers relaxing after a patrol. The Clyde remained* Archer's *home port and she continued her escort work until 1944.*

During the long campaign against the U-boat, the Firth of Clyde was ideally suited to marshalling large numbers of ships, and the Clyde naval base controlled the movements of the convoys, as it was to handle the transatlantic

Plate 31

troopship arrivals later in the war. It was also the port that received German survivors of the *Bismarck*, together with some of the triumphant British victors of that engagement, including the battleship HMS *Rodney*. (Admiral Angus Cunninghame Graham recounted how the captain of the giant British capital ship had relaxed by playing a set or two of tennis at his house at Ardoch, which looked downriver to the Tail of the Bank where the *Rodney* lay at anchor.) The sinking of the German battleship put an end to the attempted strategy of mounting attacks on commercial shipping by large fast heavily armed surface ships, in addition to the swarms of U-boats.

Plate 32 (overleaf)

Defence installations sprang up all around the Firth of Greenock; first at Greenock (referred to as 'A Northern Port' in censored communications), and after the entrance of the USA into the war, an American base on the western shore of the Gareloch, 'United States Navy Base Two', built by American personnel and used by both the US Navy and the Royal Navy.

One Clydesider's war – Part I

The plates of HMS Archer *come from the album of Lieut-Cdr Tom Wilson RNR from Dumbarton, one of the officers. He preserved in his scrapbook this poem which illustrates the pride the crew took in* Archer's *achievements:*

> *Out on the high seas her hour struck,*
> *The hour of her glorious victory.*
> *At the heart of the foe she aimed her bow*
> *With a depth-charge of thund'rous cannonry.*
>
> *Our gallant ship released her fire*
> *The ocean rocked with sound,*
> *O'er shadowed by her wings on high*
> *Her aim its home had found.*
>
> *The deadly U-boat with effort rose,*
> *One glance revealed her doom.*
> *A mighty spray, machine-guns played –*
> *She sank in her watery tomb.*

More of what was a remarkably varied naval career emerge in the plates that follow. Archer *was his last of four ships in which he served in the Supplies or Pay Section. His first ship – one which had a rather different sort of experience in the Battle of the Atlantic – was HMS* Forfar, *which he joined when she was in the Clyde in December 1939 as a writer in the pay office.* Forfar *was an armed merchant cruiser; in her former life she was the CPR liner* Montrose. **Plate 32** *shows her before she was fitted with four 6-inch guns on either side and took up convoy escort duties in the Atlantic. A*

year after Tom joined Forfar *she was torpedoed and sunk in mid-ocean in December 1940. A direct hit in the engine-room was followed by explosions from four other 'tin fish'. More than 100 lives were lost but Tom was among those survivors fortunate enough to be picked up by an old tramp steamer, itself a straggler from an eastbound convoy.*

One Clydesider's war – Part II

Returning to the Clyde Tom Wilson next joined a ship that was also to be on the receiving end of enemy action. She was a somewhat nondescript vessel known as HMS Malvernian *which operated as an anti-contraband boarding vessel, mainly in the Bay of Biscay. Her demise came not from submarine attack but from an aerial bombing delivered by the much-feared Focke–Wulf long-range bomber. Put out of action by two direct hits she drifted for nineteen days before being abandoned by the crew, as seen in* **plate 33**. *This is a final shot taken from a fishing boat which rescued Tom. Some of the crew – Tom Wilson included – were picked up and taken to neutral Spain.* **Plate 34** *shows* Malvernian *launching a boat. When they were able to return to the UK Tom next joined a minelayer HMS* Port-Quebec (**plate 35**), *his 'first posting,' he says ruefully, 'in which the ship wasn't lost.' The minelayer was one of four in the 1st Minelaying Squadron, based at Kyle of Lochalsh, and they mined a sea area stretching from the Faroes to the Ice Barrier, protected by a screen of elderly US destroyers, each with four smokestacks or 'Four Woodbine' as they were called. Then came* Archer *from 1942 until early 1945 and then a number of shore postings until demob. In a sense then, Tom Wilson's active naval career began and ended with contrasting views of the anti-submarine war – from an armed merchant cruiser intended to protect convoys which itself became a U-boat victim, to an escort carrier hailed as the ship which turned around the anti-submarine war.*

Across the Gareloch was the British base at Faslane. It had six large berths capable of accommodating the largest naval vessels and was serviced by massive cranes shipped up from Southampton Docks. The Gareloch handled the organi-

Plate 33

Plate 34

sation and loading of convoys. There was a US submarine squadron (Submarine Squadron 50 with its tender, USS *Beaver*) and, crucially, the loch provided training and supplies for Allied amphibious invasion forces bound for North Africa and subsequently the D-Day Normandy beaches. The Clyde also sent out minesweepers – some of them converted Clyde steamers – to clear the approaches to Britain's shores, and the entrance to the river was protected by a

Plate 35

boom at the Cloch lighthouse. The boom was never breached and, within its protective barrier, the Gareloch and the Clyde provided the safest of anchorages.

There were Firth of Clyde bases outside the boom. They included Rothesay Bay where there was a training establishment, through which passed 90 per cent of Britain's wartime submarine crews, including the brave men who took their midget submarines into the fjord where the *Tirpitz* was hidden away. Rothesay was also the home port for the 7th Submarine Flotilla with its depot ship HMS *Cyclops*.

More warships in the Clyde

Another escort aircraft carrier, HMS Battler *(also US built), is seen in* **plate 36**. *Other Swordfish planes are being manoeuvered around by the deck crew – in this view the nose of the torpedo can be glimpsed below the fuselage. As previously mentioned, the Swordfish torpedo bombers were seen as*

Plate 36

'sub-killers'. They had also, however, played an important role in the events surrounding the battleship
Bismarck.

The Bismarck

Events far from the Clyde had had their impact on the river. When the German battleship Bismarck *accompanied by the heavy cruiser* Prince Eugen *broke out into the Atlantic and sank the Clyde-built battle-cruiser HMS* Hood *off Greenland with the loss of all but three of her crew of 1421 on 24 May 1941 a massive concentration of British ships was assembled to deal with her. Athough the* Prince Eugen *made a safe return to the French port of Brest the* Bismarck *was finally destroyed on 27 May.*

Plate 37 shows the Hood *with attendant tugs following her launch at John Brown's yard in 1918. She carried an impressive armament of six 15-inch guns. However,* Hood *was laid down just before the Battle of Jutland and was consequently twenty years out of date at the time of her encounter with the* Bismarck.

Plate 38 shows a wounded survivor from the Bismarck *being helped ashore at Greenock by British soldiers.*

Plate 39 shows some of the other 110 captured Bismarck *survivors for whom the war was over. Another five survivors were rescued by a German submarine and a German weather ship but 2106 of her crew died, including her Captain and the commander of the German squadron, Admiral Lütjens. Plate 40 shows some of the leading British commanders, pictured together having arrived in the Clyde to refuel after the hunt for the* Bismarck. *On the left is Captain F. H. G. Dalrymple-Hamilton of the battleship HMS* Rodney, *whose 16-inch shells devastated the German ship. In the centre is Captain H. C. Bovell, of the newly commissioned aircraft carrier HMS* Victorious, *whose torpedo attack by Swordfish biplanes on the* Bismarck, *though of limited effectiveness, was the first aerial attack on a battleship at sea. A later attack by the air group from HMS* Ark Royal *damaged* Bismarck's *steering gear and allowed the British battle squadron to catch up with her. On the right is Rear Admiral W. F. Wake-Walker, Flag Officer, 1st Cruiser Squadron. Admiral Wake-Walker, flying his flag in the heavy cruiser HMS* Norfolk, *had been patrolling the Denmark Strait in company with HMS* Suffolk *and had found the* Bismarck *and shadowed her using the newly installed radar equipment.* Norfolk *was in at the kill, after the battleships* Rodney *and* King George V *had been forced to break off engagement with the sinking* Bismarck *due to lack of fuel, and had shelled and torpedoed the ruined German ship.*

Upstream from where the Clyde widens into the firth, the riverbanks were lined by the world-famous shipyards. Twice within the space of twenty-five years a wartime government ordered immediate intensification of shipbuilding and warship-building programmes, as the yards worked overtime to make up for the many years of inactivity during the Depression. Ship-repairing and the work of adaptation – carriers and the like – were also vital and in a way this work was more important than producing new ships, whose fitting-out and trials might be

Plate 37

awkward in wartime. Throughout, the Clyde was hard at work replacing and
strengthening Britain's merchant marine as the U-boats took their toll.

Plate 38 (opposite)

Plate 39 (above)

A particular feature of the Clyde in wartime was the pressing into service of
the ubiquitous river-steamers. In both wars some Clyde vessels were retained to
run restricted passenger services and for use as tenders to ships loading at the
Tail of the Bank and elsewhere in the Clyde area. Many others were called up for
war service. The table on p.72 shows the war service of a representative
selection of Clyde passenger vessels. Some, such as the *Duchess of Fife*, served in
both wars and returned to peacetime service – a tribute to the 'Clyde-built'
tradition.

Plate 40

Plate 41

Vessel	WW1	WW2	Notes
PS *Duchess of Hamilton* (1890)	Requisitioned as troopship February 1915 then served as minesweeper		Sunk by a mine November 1915
PS *Neptune* (1892)	Requisitioned as minesweeper December 1915		Renamed HMS *Napaulin*. Sunk by a mine April 1917
PS *Waverley* (1899)	Requisitioned as minesweeper November 1915	Requisitioned as minesweeper September 1939	Bombed and sunk at Dunkirk May 1940
TrSS *King Edward* (1901)	Requisitioned as troopship – served mostly between England and France. Also served as ambulance transport in White Sea area	Requisitioned as troopship and used until 1943	
PS *Duchess of Fife* (1903)	Requisitioned as minesweeper March 1916	Requisitioned as minesweeper November 1939. Served at Dunkirk. Later used as anti-aircraft training vessel on the Forth	
TrSS *Queen Alexandra* (1912)	Requisitioned for transport duties February 1915	Accommodation vessel at East India Harbour, Greenock for boom defences	
PS *Jeanie Deans* (1931)		Requisitioned as minesweeper October 1939 then used as anti-aircraft ship in Thames	
TSS *Duchess of Hamilton* (1932)		Requisitioned for use as troopship between Stranraer and Larne	
PS *Caledonia* (1934)		Requisitioned as minesweeper November 1939 then used as anti-aircraft ship	Renamed HMS *Goatfell*
PS *Mercury* (1934)		Requisitioned as minesweeper September 1939	Sunk by a mine off Irish coast December 1940
DEPV *Talisman* (1935)		Requisitioned as anti-aircraft ship August 1940	Renamed HMS *Aristo-crat*. Served as HQ ship for Mulberry Harbour
TSMV *Royal Scotsman* (1936)		Requisitioned as store carrier October 1940, later converted to Landing Ship	Served in landings in North Africa, Sicily, Italy and Normandy
PS *Jupitor* (1937)		Requisitioned as minesweeper October 1939, later served as an anti-aircraft ship in Thames and at Mulberry Harbours	Renamed HMS *Scawfell*

The war beneath the waves

In **plate 41** *a British submarine P614 comes into the Clyde in July 1942 at the conclusion of a mission in which it took part in the sinking of the German U-boat U457, which had earlier attacked an Allied convoy. Note the Jolly Roger. Officers and men are seen grouped on the foredeck, where the submarine's single gun is situated. Also on this voyage, P614 put a torpedo into a US merchant ship – member of the convoy – which earlier had been disabled by the U-boat.* **Plate 42** *shows another submarine, on this occasion a Soviet one, moored at Greenock. The submarine is a long way from its home port of Vladivostock. It has evidently come into the Clyde at some point after the Soviet Union joined the Allies in 1941 and serves as a reminder that for a considerable period of the war the Clyde was the only safe haven in the North Atlantic. Note the sailors' V-sign, in imitation of Winston Churchill's 'V for Victory' gesture, although only the officer next to the conning tower hass got it right!*

Organising the convoys

Another famous Second World War image taken by James Hall (**plate 43** *) shows ships assembled at the Tail of the Bank on the River Clyde waiting for convoy duty.* **Plate 44** *is a glimpse of the naval communications headquarters known as 'Signal City' as it was in October 1942. This station handled communications for the whole Clyde area and the Western Approaches. It was situated in a large house at a secret location somewhere in the Greenock area – probably at a villa, 'Marymount', situated high above Gourock pier. Dozens of wireless telephonists, cipher officers, teleprinter operators and dispatch riders were based there. Coding and decoding were carried on, hundreds of messages sent and received – it was at one time the busiest naval communications station outside the Admiralty. Points to note include the propaganda poster of the Spitfire in a dogfight, the Low cartoon, and the Wrens wearing the French Roll hairdo, then at its most fashionable.*

Other poignant memories of the Clyde in wartime come from accidents that affected ships, although not through direct enemy action. On the afternoon of Saturday 27 March 1943 occurred one of the biggest British naval catastrophes in home waters. Between Ardrossan and the Isle of Arran the converted escort aircraft carrier HMS *Dasher* blew up and sank in less than five minutes when one of her Swordfish planes, which were practising take-off and landing, misjudged a landing and crashed into a store of fuel and explosives. Three hundred and fifty-eight of the crew were lost, although watchers from the shore who arrived in small boats managed to rescue another one hundred and forty-nine.

Plate 42

Plate 43 (overleaf)

Plate 44

An assortment of Clyde vessels

*All sorts of vessels were pressed into service; in the Imperial War Museum's photographic records this launch (**plate 45**) is described as a 'hospital ship'. The fortunes of war brought many ships to the Clyde including vessels from countries occupied by German forces. **Plate 46** shows a group of coasters beached at Gourock – the two nearest ones have Dutch mercantile ensigns at their sterns*

Plate 45

and the vessel closest to the camera can be identified as the Rotterdam-registered coaster Oud
Beyerland.

Plate 46

The Clyde saw many troopships and supply ships enter and leave, with the Gareloch being a
major stores loading port for overseas operations while most troopships loaded at King George V dock
on the south bank of the Clyde in Glasgow. The 14 500-ton Tegelberg, **plate 47**, a Dutch liner
built in 1937 for service between Holland and the Dutch East Indies, was converted, like many others
of her kind, to trooping and brought back the men of the 4th Armoured Brigade from the
Mediterranean theatre of operations to the Clyde in February 1944. She had earlier served in the
Torch landings in North Africa. Two assault landing craft can be seen hanging in davits and iron
rungs have been built into her side for troops to use in loading the landing craft.

A familiar sight on the pre-war Clyde was the Burns and Laird vessel Royal Scotsman (**plate
48**) sailing on the route between Glasgow and Belfast. Launched in 1936, TSMV Royal Scotsman
had a useful speed of 18 knots and was taken up for service as a store carrier in October 1940. She
was later converted to a Landing Ship and, like her sister-ship, Royal Ulsterman, served in
landings in North Africa, Sicily, Italy and Normandy. She is seen here in wartime grey in the Clyde,
with a dual-purpose gun mounted on her fo'csle and an anti-aircraft gun on a raised platform at her
stern. Assault landing craft hang in davits at her side. Note the anti-shrapnel defence around her
bridge and wheelhouse.

Plate 47

Plate 48

Plate 49 is of the Clyde steamer, Jupiter, *one of several Clyde vessels with an impressive Second World War record. Three years after her launch in 1937 she was turned into a minesweeper, sailing under the wartime name of* HMS Scawfell. *This plate probably shows* Jupiter *in her next role, as an anti-aircraft aircraft ship involved in escort duties. Her final manifestation was as a support vessel in the (largely Clyde-built) Mulberry Harbours in the Normandy landings.*

Plate 50 is of the rather older diesel-engined Clyde steamer, Talisman. *She too, saw war service*

Plate 49

Plate 50

as an anti-aircraft ship in waters as far as the Mediterranean, when she sailed in support of the Torch landings in North Africa. Talisman – renamed HMS Aristocrat – was also a command ship in the Mulberry Harbours.

Plate 51

The provision of new warships on the Clyde sometimes reflected the Admiralty's preoccupations and even prejudices. Not even by 1939 had the weakness of a naval strategy based on the primacy of the battleship been fully appreciated. The realisation that the aircraft carrier was the capital ship of the future was slow to dawn on Britain (the *Implacable* and the *Indefatigable* were Clyde-built carriers but were not ready until the war was already under way) and not at all on Germany. At the outbreak of war battleships still featured largely in order books, although there were several cancellations and the Clyde only completed the *Duke of York* and the *Howe* in the duration. (The *Vanguard* wasn't completed until 1947 and never fired a shot in anger.)

Shipbuilding up to the 1930s

*This drawing by Muirhead Bone (**plate 51**) is of the launch of HMS Argonaut at Fairfield's yard on 24 January 1898.*

Although the Clyde had been a prominent naval shipbuilding centre

Plate 52

Plate 53

for many years before the outbreak of the First World War, the Clyde area was less well developed as a centre for other forms of arms and armaments manufacture. The principal firm in this trade was William Beardmore's, whose Parkhead Forge plant began manufacturing guns and armour plate around 1886. In 1905 the company created a new shipyard on a greenfield site at Dalmuir, Clydebank, adjacent to the yard of John Brown. This new yard was designed primarily as a warship yard and reflected the growing international arms race and the demand for ever-larger and more powerful battleships. **Plate 52** *shows the fitting-out basin at Dalmuir with the last of the Royal Navy's pre-Dreadnought battleships HMS Agamemnon (16 500 tons, four 12-inch and ten 9.2-inch guns) completing her construction. She had been launched in 1906. She lies beside the Imperial Russian Navy's armoured cruiser Rurik (15 000 tons, four 10-inch and eight 8-inch guns.) The Rurik had been built in England by Vickers and came to the Clyde to be completed. The design of the heavily armoured Rurik reflected some of the lessons Russia had learned in the Russo-Japanese War of 1904–5 and their naval defeat at Tsushima. With the coming of the First World War Dalmuir became a production naval yard with battleships such as HMS Ramillies and many smaller vessels being built. Production also stepped up at Parkhead, where guns of all types were manufactured.* **Plate 53** *shows a week's production of 4-inch naval guns from the Forge. The 4-inch gun was fitted as main armament on destroyers and other small vessels and as secondary armament on cruisers and battleships.*

The USA and in particular Japan did give greater emphasis to the aircraft carrier, recognising the tremendous flexibility and hitting power they gave operating far from land air-bases. On the other hand, as we have seen, Germany did learn the lesson of the submarine's importance from the First World War, giving it a high priority and almost winning the Battle of the Atlantic.

A main contribution made by the Clyde to the British submarine arm was torpedo manufacture. This began before the First World War at Greenock at the Royal Navy Torpedo Factory. Between the wars manufacture also started up at the old Argyll car works in Alexandria while the Experiment and Design facilities were concentrated at Greenock. The Royal Ordnance Works at Dalmuir and at Ardeer were among those producing other kinds of explosive weapons. Meanwhile, shipbuilding down the Firth at the Ardrossan yard supplemented the major effort in the upper river as can be seen in this summary of the variety of wartime activity.

Ardrossan in the First World War brought orders for Admiralty vessels including minesweepers and a large stern-wheeler, and HMS *Pactolus* was placed at the harbour to care for a squadron of submarines which, together with other ships, were repaired and refitted by Ardrossan shipyard. To refuel the submarines, one of the piers was modified to become a small tanker berth, and fuel tanks together with the necessary pipelines and pumps were installed.

In the Second World War, Ardrossan was taken over by the Admiralty and named HMS *Fortitude*. All passenger services from the port were suspended, but ferries sailed from Fairlie. Between the wars the number of employees at the shipyard had declined, but at that time about 700 men were kept busy and twenty-five new ships built, including minesweeping trawlers and boom defence vessels. There was also a vast amount of repair work: forty-nine submarines, thirty-one destroyers, ten frigates and also eight corvettes were repaired or refitted in addition to another 359 Admiralty vessels and 288 merchant ships.

So the Clyde was crucial to the war effort both as a port, especially between 1939–45, and as a builder of naval power in both wars.

Shipbuilding from the 1930s

Britain ended the First World War with a huge fleet (including around sixty battleships and battle-cruisers) and a substantial naval building programme. Much of this programme was scrapped and for the 1920s and much of the 1930s naval building was at a low ebb because of financial stringency, an international attempt to cap naval building programmes (the Washington Naval Agreement) and a domestic policy that held as a planning presumption that there would be no war for ten years – a measure that lasted until 1932. **Plate 54** *shows one of the results of the rearmament policy of the mid-1930s – the cruiser HMS Glasgow being moved into Scott's fitting-out basin in Greenock after her launch on 20 June 1936 by Mrs Baldwin, the Prime Minister's wife. Glasgow was a light*

Plate 54

cruiser of the Southampton *class, of 9100 tons displacement and mounting twelve 6-inch guns,*
although in the course of the war one of the after triple 6-inch turrets was removed and replaced
with additional anti-aircraft guns – a reflection of the increasing threat from the air. Scott's yard
would build another four cruisers for the Royal Navy in the pre-war and wartime period – HMS
Scylla, Bonaventure, Royalist *and* Defence *– as well as a large number of smaller vessels,*
especially submarines which were something of a speciality of the yard. The battleship HMS Howe
is seen in **plate 55** *being towed down the Clyde in 1942, with tugs fore and aft from Fairfield's yard*
at Govan. The riverbanks are lined with workers and spectators of all ages, and over all is that air of
pride in workmanship that has not altogether vanished from Clydeside. Tom Gallacher wrote in his
memories of a wean growing up beside the river seeing the great ships:

'They towered above us. The sand under our bare feet trembled to the vibration of their engines. Yelling and waving we pranced about. They were OUR ships. Their engine rooms were manned by OUR uncles and brothers and cousins.'

Plate 55

HMS Howe *was a battleship, one of the five vessels of the* King George V *class, all built by Fairfield. Some indication of the size and complexity of these vessels is given by her building time:*

Ordered	*1937 Naval Estimates*
Laid down	*1 June 1937*
Launched	*9 April 1940*
Completed	*29 August 1942*

Not all of the men of the Clyde were in the forces – many of the shipyard workers were in reserved occupations and the strikes and other forms of industrial action that were in peacetime so much a feature of the yards were reduced even if not completely abandoned: for example, the 'tuppence an hour' strike in 1915 and the strike in John Brown's yard, which was brought to an abrupt conclusion by the Clydebank blitz of March 1941.

Like many politically aware workers throughout the country, Clydesiders threw their effort wholeheartedly into the war effort, partly through straightforward patriotism, but partly because they saw themselves as part of an

Plate 56

international movement against fascism, standing alongside their distant Soviet allies, as well as the ever-present 'Yanks'.

An American view

Plate 56 and 57, *taken on 30 April 1942, show unnamed ships at the Tail of the Bank, one of which is carrying landing craft, or 'barges' as the Americans called them, athwart the ship. It is likely that this is an early manifestation of the great build-up to Operation Torch in October of the same year.*

Plates 57

The US National Archives indicate that these two plates were in fact taken by this aircraft
carrier, USS Wasp, which was in the Clyde in April 1942, very soon after the USA entered the war
in December 1941. **Plate 58** shows the Wasp, of 18 000 tons, part of a British–US force which,
at Churchill's request, was sent to the Mediterranean with a complement of Hurricanes – she could
carry up to eighty aircraft – to assist the valiant defenders in the siege of Malta. She was later sunk
in the Pacific.

Plate 58

CHAPTER 3

War in the air

Whenever there's a raid on, you'll hear me cry,
'An airyplane, an airyplane, away-way up a-ky!'
You'll run helter-skelter, don't run after me,
You'll no' get in ma shelter, for it's far too wee.

Dave Willis

Plate 59
German Junkers 88s in formation.

The first wave of German bombers took off from the airfields of the Luftwaffe's Third Air Fleet in western France as evening fell on 13 March 1941. The bombers were Heinkel 111s, and they were carrying a payload of high-explosive (HE) bombs as well as flares and incendiaries as they followed the radio navigation beam. They were closely followed by other groups of Heinkels and Junkers 88s (also twin-engined bombers and capable of being adapted to a fighter role). The Junkers was generally regarded as a more effective machine than the Heinkel – together they carried out all of the raids on western Scotland in the spring of 1941. As they came in over the North Sea, the sirens wailed as it became clear that the 'targets for tonight' included Clydeside. This was the way that aerial war first came to the towns along the riverbanks.

The fear of death delivered from the air had grown in the years since the last war – a war in which the only air action seen in Scotland had been a raid by Zeppelins over the Forth. The destruction of cities like Guernica in the Spanish Civil War and other fascist bombing atrocities were still fresh in people's minds. Most military theorists argued that the next war would be won quickly and decisively by a sudden or 'lightning' onslaught – an intense aerial bombardment of cities and their civilian populations, paralysing their communications and industrial bases. Poison gas would probably be used (hence the carrying of gas masks). It was an article of faith that 'the bomber will always get through'.

First World War aviation

Even before the First World War Beardmore had diversified into aero-engine building, constructing Austro-Daimler engines under licence from 1913. As the First World War progressed the Beardmore enterprise became an even more widely diversified armaments manufacturer with the company delivering their first aircraft, a BE2C, in March 1915. Their works at Dalmuir, Dumbartonshire, were

Plate 60

the centre of production for aircraft like this and the Sopwith Pup seen in **plate 60**. The company developed an airfield at Inchinnan in Renfrewshire which became their centre for airship production. The Sopwith Pup came into production in 1916 and proved to be a highly successful fighter aircraft, popular with pilots because of its splendid handling characteristics. A tiny aircraft with a wingspan of only 26.5 feet and weighing only 1225 pounds, its 80-horsepower Le Rhône rotary engine gave it a top speed of 111 m.p.h. The Beardmore factory and the Sopwith factory together turned out around 1700 Pups. Note the .303 Vickers machine-gun mounted above the upper wing. A Sopwith Pup was the first aircraft to land on a moving ship – HMS Furious – in 1917.

The Germans had shown the usefulness of the airship and Zeppelins had raided Britain's east coast. Britain, too, developed the airship and the R34, built by Beardmore's at the end of the war, might have had a military role but her first flight did not take place until 20 December 1918. R34, pictured in **plate 61** at Inchinnan, was driven by five 250-horse power motors and makes a striking contrast to the Sopwith Pup. She was 643 feet long and the total volume of her gas-filled bag was 1 950 000 cubic feet. Speed was not the main quality of the airship – the R34 flew at a stately 54 m.p.h. – but long range and endurance certainly was. In July 1919 the R34 left the East Fortune *airfield in East Lothian and flew to New York in just over 108 hours. A few days later she recrossed the Atlantic, this time in 75 hours with the aid of westerly winds, and landed in Norfolk. Sadly the R34 was destroyed in an accident in 1921. The huge airship sheds seen in the background were demolished in the 1930s when a rubber factory was built on the Inchinnan site. Many Clyde shipbuilders diversified into aircraft production during the First World War with, for example, Denny of Dumbarton manufacturing 150 BE2Cs. Beardmore, however, also developed their own design capacity and continued their aviation involvement after the war by operating the RAF Reserve Flying School at Renfrew between 1923 and 1928.*

The initial impression left by the early German attacks on Poland seemed to confirm this conviction, but by the time of the Clydeside raids in March and May of 1941, everyone had seen London's resilience in the face of the bombing of late 1940. From the evidence of that it seemed that this was not going to be a 'lightning war' or blitzkrieg as it was termed in German. Nevertheless, although it was to be much more of a war of attrition, the name stuck and 'blitz' became everyone's word for the bombing raids.

Plate 61

The Second World War – The raiders

Plate 62 (previous page)

Three Junkers 88 A-type bombers, as commonly used in raids on Clydeside, are seen flying in
formation in **plate** 62. *The bomb-load was extensive (bombs were carried under the wings and*
fuselage). The crew of four was grouped together in the forward area: the pilot higher on the port
side, the bomb-aimer lower in the nose and the upper rear gunner behind the pilot. The radio operator
also operated the lower rear gun in the blister which can be seen underneath on the starboard side.
The Junkers 88 was among the most effective of all the Second World War German bombers and
remained in production in many different forms and in operation throughout the period of hostilities.
The other type of aircraft employed in the German raids was the Heinkel E111. **Plate** 63 *is a*
German air reconnaissance plate of the 'seaport' of Greenock used by bomber missions, during the
raids of 6 and 7 May 1941. Several hundred aircraft are believed to have taken part in the raids,
with the planes operating at a height of 12 000 feet. Over 500 tons of high explosive and 2500
incendiary canisters were carried. The military and commercial nature of the enemy intentions can be
seen with targets such as the docks, fuel tanks and supply depots being listed. As will be seen, the
proximity of these targets to heavily populated areas, and the large number of incendiaries dropped

Plate 63

resulted in extensive casualties (as had been the case two months earlier in Clydebank and Glasgow *where over 1200 had died). More than 300 were killed at Greenock.*

The German aircraft carried flares and three main types of bomb:

- incendiaries which set targets ablaze and acted as a beacon to following planes
- high-explosive bombs
- parachute mines – sometimes wrongly called landmines, which were designed to explode close to the ground, thus providing a great deal of lateral blast.

On the lookout for the attacking force that night in March were night-fighters, mostly from Turnhouse airfield, and other air-defence measures included balloon defences at Glasgow and Renfrew, searchlights and heavy anti-aircraft guns ('Ack-Ack guns' in popular parlance). Radar counter-measures – a technological breakthrough inspired by a Scot, Sir Robert Watson-Watt – were in use though not as elaborate nor as effective as they would become. Also elaborate and most effective was the system of decoy fires and lights known by the codename Starfish. These decoys were installed in the vicinity of prime targets like the port of the Clyde and were intended to draw attacking bombers away from the real targets and into areas where their bombs would be harmless to industry and to the population at large. As soon as the raids began, a small force of servicemen, showing great courage, lit fires in the hills above the river – the effectiveness of Starfish was shown when, in the light of day, a large number of bomb craters were discovered in these same hills. Bombing was an inexact science compared with what it would become later in the war and, although there was a 'pathfinder' unit among the enemy planes, some of the German aircraft dropped their bombs indiscriminately and wide of target. The industrial damage was not excessive. Dr I.M.M. MacPhail, historian of the Clydebank blitz and himself a veteran of bomb disposal units, described the first Clydebank raid:

Rivers and railways showed clearly to aircraft 12 000 feet above. According to the secret and confidential report from the Luftwaffe Headquarters next day, conditions were favourable to the attacking aircraft both in regard to weather and visibility; not only could the target areas be clearly identified but, it was claimed, the crews could distinguish the craters made by the bombs. In the report it was stated that 'from 22.30 hours to 06.47 hours (21.30 to 05.47 by British time) 236 bombers attacked along the length of the River Clyde with about 272 tons of high-explosive bombs and 1650 incendiary containers.'

The defenders

Balloon defences were deployed with the intention of counteracting bombing raids, particularly those at low level. There were balloon squadrons at Glasgow, Renfrew and Ardrossan, although balloons were also installed at Greenock and elsewhere – it should be noted that enemy aircraft such as the Junkers 88 could be fitted with balloon cable-cutters or fenders. In **plate 64** a group of sailors is seen manoeuvering a balloon, two of them being lifted off their feet. Next, in **plate 65**, a Hawker Sea Hurricane is seen on a steam catapult fitted to a CAM (catapult-equipped merchantman) in 1943. The pilot can be seen next to the sliding cockpit cover. A shipboard fighter such as this could extend the area within which ships could be given fighter protection from enemy aircraft or U-boat attack. Obviously, the aircraft would have to return to a shore base after being in action and therefore was inferior to carrier-borne aircraft. The CAMs were introduced in 1941 and the first enemy aircraft to be destroyed by a catapulted Sea Hurricane was shot down on 3 August 1941. Along with the Spitfire, the Hurricane is the plane most associated with the defence of the UK against German bombing raids. From 1941 on, Fighter Command were instructed to treat the Clyde, the Mersey and the Bristol Channel as number one priorities for defence – accordingly, increasing numbers of fighter squadrons were located in the Clyde area. The Sea Hurricane was a version of one of the most versatile British aircraft of the period, which served on a total of seventeen battlefronts – and

Plate 64

Hurricanes particularly distinguished themselves in the defence of Malta (some sailed from the Clyde on USS Carrier Wasp*). The Sea Hurricane was fitted with catapult spools and deck arrester gear for aircraft carrier use.*

Plate 65

These statistics may seem small compared with Allied bomb-loads during the saturation bombing of Germany, but the suffering of Clydebank people was irrefutable and is clearly described by Dr MacPhail in *The Clydebank Blitz*:

Most of the fatal casualties in Clydebank occurred as a result of the explosion of bombs and mines, either directly by blast or by the collapse of the building in which people sheltered. Hardly one street in the burgh was without a fatal casualty but some streets were affected worse than others. Second Avenue, where a direct hit 'pulled the face off second Terrace' . . . and brought the whole front of the building down, was the street with the highest number of fatal casualties – altogether 80 deaths at Nos. 72 to 78 and 159 to 163. They included ten of the Diver family in No. 76 and eight of the McSherry family at No. 161 . . .

It was in 78 Jellicoe Street that fifteen members of the Rocks family perished, the most grievous tragedy of the whole blitz in Clydebank; and to the present day the notice by the survivors of the families in the 'In Memoriam' columns of the *Clydebank Press* brings back recollections of that night of terror in Jellicoe Street.

Plate 66 (previous page)

Further raids up and down the Clyde took place in April and these were followed by a major attack on Greenock on 6 and 7 May, in which considerable damage was done. An emergency edition of the Greenock local paper ran this under the headline 'Scots town blitzed' (the censor could demand that no direct reference be made to a strategically significant port or other sensitive location).

One of the most intensive raids in Britain was launched on Clydeside on Tuesday night. HE and incendiaries dropped on centre of one town over prolonged period. Much damage due to fires.

As with Clydebank, there was evidence that Greenock actually had civil defence procedures in place and working (even if pacifist and left-wing local politicians had resisted these until almost the last moment). These procedures were on the whole more efficient and responsive than had been the case in parts of England earlier in the war. The Ministry of Home Security had set up an HQ in Glasgow and 102 Rest Centres and Air Raid Warden posts had been established in strategic locations. The newspaper account continued:

Defence services, aided by personnel of the armed forces, did magnificent work in rescuing buried people and extinguishing fires. All worked heroically even at height of blitz. High praise for defence workers in a blitzed Scots town was paid by Sir Stephen Bilsland, Civil Defence Commissioner. 'Wardens and messengers (boys and girls) delivered messages throughout severity of raid with wonderful determination. If there is lesson to be learned from this raid, it is that local authorities must not only be satisfied that their rest centres and organisation for homeless look well on paper but that they can come into action in stress and work under difficulties. If raiding in western districts has been later than elsewhere, we should be the better prepared to deal with it.'

The May 1941 raids – Part I

The bombing raids on the moonlit nights of 13 and 14 March (a 'bomber's moon') are remembered locally as the Clydebank blitz, because of the tremendous impact on that burgh, even though many bombs fell on the same nights on Glasgow. More than 1200 people were killed and more than 1000 seriously injured on the two nights of bombing, although it seems clear that the Germans had targeted the shipyards and factories rather than people's homes.

The astonishing thing about the Clydeside blitz of 1941 is that it lasted so short a time. Two nights in March saw Clydebank and areas of Glasgow receive the heaviest punishment – then two months later it was the turn of Greenock on the nights of 6 and 7 May. On their way to bomb Greenock, however, some bombs were dropped on Dumbarton and the little village of Cardross, on the north bank of the river. **Plate 66**, taken from the back-court area, shows a bombed tenement in Glasgow Road, Dumbarton. Members of the ARP and rescue squads can be seen picking through the bombsite, which shows the effect of extreme blast, probably from a parachute mine. Poignant remnants of people's homes (several people died in this incident) include the clock on the wall of one room and the kitchen water heater on another, on either side of the gap.

This drawing (**plate 67**) was done soon after the raid on 6 May 1941, by 17-year-old Jim Adie who witnessed attacking German planes unloading a large quantity of incendiary and HE bombs on the village of Cardross. The drawing is an impression of the view from the verandah of Cardross Golf Clubhouse (where he lived) showing the 18th fairway peppered with incendiaries – the remnants of more than 500 of these were found in the vicinity and the clubhouse itself was completely destroyed by fire, despite the valiant efforts of Jim and his mother to save their home.

Plate 67

Another general point which would be equally true of any of the areas of Clydeside which underwent bombing raids is this: while there was, rightly, some satisfaction that civil defence was well planned and responsive, much of this was due to the bravery and initiative of individuals. In the Clydebank blitz, too, senior pupils from local schools provided invaluable assistance as messengers (and voluntary firewatchers on the roofs of public buildings). The ability of people to keep morale high and spirits buoyant is something that shines through even such bald and factual accounts as this:

In districts where transport upset by blitz, Home Office asks all car-owners to help by offering lifts to walkers. Arrangements for the re-housing of homeless families are proceeding apace. Some bombed-out families have already left town for evacuation areas – others accommo-dated with friends. Town officials, with assistance from Regional Commissioner's office, schoolteachers, and other voluntary workers, worked long hours at rest centres to relieve distress . . . First-aid repairs to business premises and houses have begun. Many shops have not shut their doors since blitz. Customers have been served from windowless premises. 'We have now more open space to work in,' said notice outside one shop.

Mention was made of the rescue services and the part played by volunteers, many from outside the affected areas, like the West Lothian miners who came through to the west coast when they heard the news of the blitz on Clydebank:

They arrived on the Friday and were sent to deal with the results of an explosion in Mount Blow . . . They had built for themselves a hut out of pieces of timber and when discovered they were brewing up some tea before going on to another job. When told about the message from the burgh surveyor, they replied that they would return when they heard that their own town had been bombed and that they were required, but otherwise they would stay as long as they were needed in Clydebank. These miners had a different technique from the other rescue parties, which generally tackled the rescue of buried people by standing on top of the debris and gradually throwing it off, whereas the miners con-structed a little tunnel, about two feet high, from the street through the wall of the building and thereby got into the centre of the debris . . .

The Clydebank Blitz

This was the time when any remaining feeling that this was simply to be a 'phoney war' was abandoned. From a stock of 12 000 houses in Clydebank, for example, a mere seven were undamaged and overnight the population actually remaining in their own homes plummeted from nearly 50 000 to 2000.

For London, the south-east and elsewhere south of the border, the awareness of the harsh reality of war had come earlier. The interesting evidence of the unique 'Mass Observation' project – which recorded the reactions of a wide cross-section of people at war – was that any notion of 'morale' had to take account of the actual local circumstances. Morale, it seemed, was also:

> influenced by the intensity of a raid and the scale and nature of the damage sustained . . . people's ability to withstand attack declined as the raids increased in frequency, or threatened to do so.

Mass Observation concluded that repetitive bombing of this kind:

> was much the hardest type of attack to get used to . . . it is very doubtful if people can condition themselves to more than three nights of intensive attack in a week.

It was fortunate for Clydeside, therefore, that the two main spells of intense bombing in the whole course of the war were months apart, in March and May of 1941. Neither of these spells individually exceeded the three-night figure, unlike the experience, for example, of the unfortunate inhabitants of Plymouth. Those Clyde towns that absorbed bombed-out refugees, such as Greenock, Paisley, Dumbarton and even the village of Cardross, also suffered in the raids, but after the Greenock blitz they virtually came to an end. Remarkably, the full force of German bombing attacks on most British cities and ports was suspended at this point. Hitler's launching of Operation Barbarossa against the Soviet Union deflected attention to the east just at the point when the raids were beginning to prove effective. Clydebank and Greenock were spared the kind of fate meted out to the likes of Hamburg and Dresden, or for that matter in the parts of the south-east of England which bore the brunt of Hitler's V-weapon attacks.

The May 1941 raids – Part II

Plate 68 *shows the scene 43–45 Belville Street, Greenock, which was hit on the first night of the Greenock blitz, that of the 6 May. In selecting Greenock as a target, the Luftwaffe intended to single out shipyards and shipping in the river as principal targets, such as Lamont's Dry Dock, seen in* **plate 69**. *Most damage was, however, done to dwelling houses and industrial buildings, like Greenock's*

Plate 68

Plate 69

famous sugar houses, rather than military targets. The town suffered even more damage the second night, that of the 7th. In **plate 70**, *smoke from the still-burning fires almost obscures the Mid Kirk in the centre of the town while workmen clear rubble from Cathcart Street. The image resembles the famous plate of St Paul's taken the year before as London burned.* **Plate 71** *shows Cathcart Street again, this time looking in a south-easterly direction at Black's Corner. The wrought-iron lamp still hangs there despite the wreckage all around. The Fire Brigade hoses are snaking everywhere – damage to the water mains meant that the firefighters had to draw water from the harbour. In* **plate 72** *there is another apocalyptic view showing smoke still rising from the buildings at Cathcart Street and Duff Street, Greenock. The wind, which during the night had fanned the conflagration, has dropped; the fires are clearly visible from miles away on the opposite bank of the Clyde. ARP (Air Raid Precautions) officers are seen among the rescue squads who were out on the streets of the town for two nights running.* **Plate 73** *shows the back green of 8 Quarrier Street in Greenock with a high-explosive bomb crater nearby. In the immediate pre-war period some politicians had been resistant to the idea of civil defence, and a Labour member of Greenock Corporation had predicted that if war came to Greenock, 'the people [will do] nothing regarding ARP shelters, but are going to take to the hills.'*

The blitz, therefore, was Clydeside's most dramatic experience of aerial warfare. Few can remember anything about the area's experience in the First World War, yet a war memorial in the form of a Celtic cross can be viewed in the village of Kirkoswald, erected by the people of the parish in 1923 to honour those airmen, British, Australian and American, stationed at Turnberry Air Field 'in the School of Aerial Gunnery and Fighting', who died in 1917 and 1918.

On the manufacturing side, the firm of Beardmore's in Dalmuir, mainly known for its warship-building, assembled large numbers of aircraft such as the Sopwith Camel (remembered as the plane flown by the fictitious air-ace Biggles) and the Sopwith Pup. Most of these rugged and 'beautifully simple' biplanes, with a maximum speed of 111 m.p.h., were destined for service with the Royal Flying Corps in France or RNAS squadrons. Altogether, Scottish firms built 4390 aircraft during the war years.

For a while, too, the assembly of airships for offensive operations was carried on by Beardmore across the river at Renfrew. The most famous of these was the R34, which was over 600 feet long and was built in response to the German Zeppelins, but did not make its first flight until December 1918. These – to our eyes – strange machines (resembling 'a Trades Hoose cigar' according to Neil Munro's humorous character, Erchie Macpherson) did not play any significant combat role in the Clyde area, although Glasgow had a blackout enforced in case of Zeppelin raids. As in the case of shipbuilding, Clydeside's primary role was to provide the weapons and equipment for waging aerial warfare.

In the next war the Clyde performed a similar function, particularly at the Blackburn Aircraft Factory in Dumbarton, where a series of planes were made for different purposes. Most successful of these were the Short Sunderland flying-boats, which in this case saw useful service on the Atlantic front. Many of the Sunderlands served in Coastal Command, on long-range reconnaissance and anti-submarine duties. Some flew from the Ardencaple Base at Helensburgh and the Firth of Clyde fell within their patrol areas. Initially, the most active land bases in the Clyde area were Turnberry, which flew Hampdens and later Lockheed Hudsons and Venturas, also on anti-submarine duties. Mention should be made of the voluntary element in air defence and in particular of 602 (City of Glasgow) Squadron of the Royal Auxiliary Air Force. This had been the first AAF Squadron to be formed in September 1925. It was originally based at Renfrew but moved to Abbotsinch in January 1933 and was equipped with Spitfires in April 1939, ahead of many regular RAF squadrons. Flying from Drem, East Lothian, 602 had its first of many encounters with German aircraft on 16 October 1939.

Plate 70

Plate 71

The May 1941 raids – Part III

Several public buildings were damaged in the Greenock bombing, although the prominent municipal buildings escaped destruction. In **plates 74 and 75** *Cartsburn Primary School and St Andrew's Square United Free Church have suffered extensive damage from incendiaries and lost their roofs. In the months and years since the outbreak of war firewatching duties were regularly carried out by volunteers, such as members of school staffs – obviously the suddenness and scale of the fires which were set burning in Greenock and Gourock rendered such precautions pointless. Further plates (***plates**

Plate 72

Plate 73

Plate 74

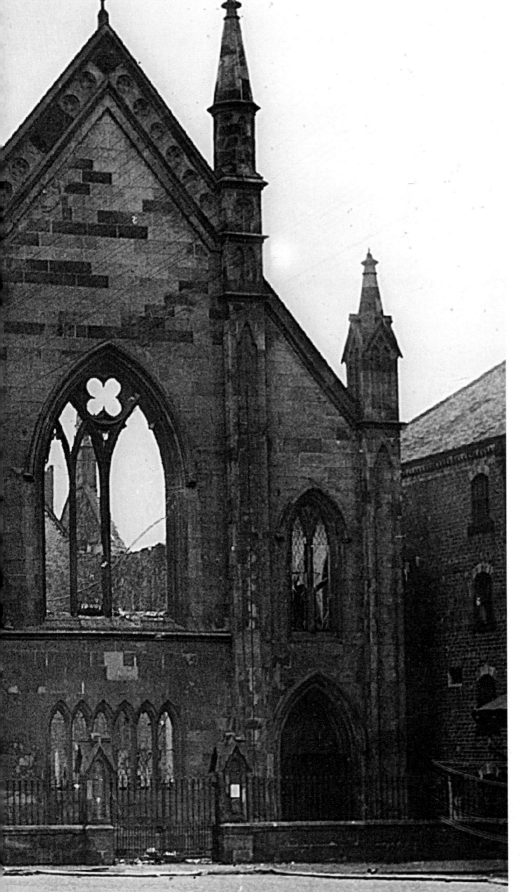

Plate 75

*76 and 77) show large-scale bomb damage at Rue End Street looking east from Dellingburn Street corner (now the location of Greenock Fire Station), while rescuers pick through rubble at Tarbet Street Corner, Gourock, in an effort to find survivors – over 300 people lost their lives over those two nights in May. A refuse lorry and builders' ladders indicate how voluntary assistance had an important part to play in the rescue operations. Finally, a plate (**plate 78**) of the Thom Street area indicates the near-obliteration of some domestic properties and another (**plate 79**) that bomb damage also affected shops and commercial properties.*

By far the most significant contribution of Clydeside to the Allied war effort in the air, however, came from the strategic power centre that was Prestwick airbase. It had opened as a civil airport in 1935 and was requisitioned for military

Plate 76

use in 1939. (At the present day it is still used as a Royal Naval Air Station, HMS *Gannet*, operating Sea King helicopters in anti-submarine warfare and search and rescue roles.)

What went on at Prestwick in the Second World War was extremely hush-hush at the time, but since the war the truth has gradually emerged about this amazingly important base. As recently as the 1930s it had only been a farmer's field. First came an RAF pilot and navigation training school, but even that was small beer to what was to follow. With the entry of the Americans and as part of an international co-operative effort involving, significantly, the Royal Canadian Air Force, runways were built and Prestwick became the main reception airfield for planes being ferried from North America to the European theatre of war. By the end of the war, for example, 400 Lancaster bombers had been built in Canada for the RAF in the works of the appropriately named Victory Aircraft Ltd. If Britain can be compared with a great aircraft carrier offshore from Europe, then Prestwick was the main flight deck. The great Prestwick airlift saw some 6000 separate flights arrive at or depart from these shores and the airfield controlled a vital air channel in the same way as the River Clyde controlled the sea channels.

For example, the USAAF 401st Bomb Group, known as 'Bowman's Bombers' – who flew B17G Flying Fortresses and were based at Deenethorpe in England from November 1943 to June 1945 – had an interesting connection with the Clyde area. They flew 255 missions to Nazi Europe with a total of 7430 sorties and a bomb tonnage of 17 778 tons. The group was formed in 1943 in Washington State. On completion of final training the ground 'echelon' began movement overseas in October 1943. The unit embarked on the *Queen Mary* at New York, sailed on the 27 October and arrived at Greenock on the 2 November 1943, disembarking the following day. The air 'echelon' (their aircraft) left on the 18 October 1943 via Goose Bay, Newfoundland and Meeks Field in Iceland to Prestwick. After VE Day they were 'redeployed' to the USA in June 1945. The air echelon departed the UK on 30 May and reached their home base on 4 June 1945. The ground echelon went by train to Gourock on 20 June, and sailed on the *Queen Elizabeth* on the 25 June 1945, arriving on the 30th, a mere five days later.

Operations such as these represented an important joint US–Canadian contribution to the war effort, for the movement of aircraft eastward utilised an integrated network of bases constructed and manned by personnel of both countries.

Plate 77

Plate 78

Plate 79 (opposite)

'The Atlantic bridge'

Elsewhere in this book the large-scale ferrying of big aircraft from Canada and the USA is described. Most of these were flown into Prestwick and in **plate 80** *we see an RAF Lancaster bomber built in Canada under licence and ferried to Scotland. The first of the Avro Lancasters was built in 1942 and the first Canadian version flown to Prestwick in September 1943. The most versatile of British heavy bombers, the Lancaster was also manufactured in Australia. It could carry a normal bomb-load of 14 000 pounds with a range of up to 1000 miles, although with modifications it could take the 12 000- or 22 000-pound monsters carried by no other bomber.* **Plate 81** *is a view of US B17 Flying Fortresses, also at Prestwick.* **Plate 82** *shows a B17 Flying Fortress refuelling from a tanker. The Boeing B17G was a version of the Fortress — powered by four Wright nine-cylinder radial air-cooled engines — thousands of which were built and used on battlefronts around the world. It carried a crew of 6–10, and in these plates we can see the plastic nose, where the bomb-aimer was located, and the 'chin' turret, where two of the aircraft's thirteen machine-guns were located; one of the two guns in 'cheek' mountings is also visible. The normal capacity of the bomb-bay was 6000 pounds.*

Plate 80

Plate 81

Plate 82

The first step in building this 'Atlantic bridge' was taken in July 1940 when the British Ministry of Aircraft Production arranged with Canadian Pacific Railway Company for the operation of a ferry service between a western terminal at Dorval Airport near Montreal and an eastern terminal at Prestwick. Aircraft were to be delivered by civilian pilots to Dorval from the plants of US aircraft manufacturers in California. The first delivery, of seven Hudsons, took place on 11 November 1940 and involved a 2100-mile hop from Newfoundland Airport to the UK. By February 1941 Boeing Flying Fortresses (B17s) and Consolidated Liberators (B24s) were also being flown over the route.

On 15 July 1941 the ferrying operation was taken over by the British Ministry of Aircraft Production itself through its ATFERO (Atlantic Ferrying Organisation). At this time 59 per cent of the pilots were American, 10 per cent Canadian, and 28 per cent British. Responsibility was next taken over by the Royal Air Force Ferry Command.

United States participation in the ferrying of aircraft produced for the UK
began shortly after approval of the initial 'lend–lease' appropriations on 27 April
1941. In early May 1941 US Army Air Corps and UK officials discussed a plan for
US assumption of the transcontinental portion of the ferrying. Britain benefited
from a reduction in the cost of delivery of the aircraft and the release of a large
number of civilian pilots who could then be employed on the transatlantic leg of
the delivery route. On 28 May President Roosevelt assigned to the War
Department the responsibility for delivery of lend–lease aircraft to the point of
take-off from the United States for the UK. In the six months preceding Pearl
Harbor, the Air Corps Ferry Command ferried 1350 aircraft to the eastern
seaboard for further movement by air or sea – some, particularly the smaller
aircraft, were sent crated on ships. Short-range aircraft were ferried to the UK
over a route through Greenland and Iceland to Prestwick. In Iceland, Britain had
constructed airfields at Reykjavik and Kaldaharnes after they established a
garrison there in 1940. In Greenland the US proceeded to garrison the island and
develop air-bases. The operations of the Air Transport Command, which had
their beginnings in 1942, reached major proportions the following year. A fleet of
some thirty-five four-engine and thirteen two-engine aircraft, mostly operated
by civilian contract carriers, carried over 7600 tons of cargo eastward and 2200
tons westward, in addition to 15 235 passengers, during 1943. After 1 September
1943 the transatlantic operations were staged principally through Harmon Field
at Stephenville, with Gander and Goose Bay Airports used as alternatives. By the
time of VE Day the Air Transport Command's North Atlantic fleet numbered
approximately 100 four-engine and sixteen two-engine transports. The smaller
aircraft such as fighters and fighter-bombers, which were crated and shipped to
the Clyde, arrived at King George V Dock and were then taken by road to
Abbotsinch where they were assembled before being flown on elsewhere.

In the air, as well as at sea, the Clyde area was a pivotal element in binding
together three great Atlantic Allies.

CHAPTER 4

Troops and troopships

He's a braw, braw Hielan laddie, Private Jock McDade.
There's not anither sodger like him in the Scotch Brigade.
Rear'd among the heather, you can see he's Scottish built,
By the wig, wig, wiggle, wiggle-waggle o' the kilt.

Harry Lauder

Plate 83
Nineteenth-century gun battery on an Argyll shore.

War is a deadly serious business of course, but the Clydesider can find humour in almost any situation. When the fictional Para Handy's inimitable cook, the Glaswegian Sunny Jim, finally managed (despite his glass eye) to enlist in the Royal Scots Fusiliers (by passing himself off as Dan Macphail the engineer), he had to report to Fort Matilda at Greenock. This meant he was able to visit his shipmates in a couple of weeks' time, and give his initial impressions of army life:

'It's a gentleman's life,' declared the young recruit. 'Naething hard aboot it, except that ye have to keep your teeth brushed. I don't think I could think o' goin' back to follow the sea when the war's past; sodgerin' puts ye aff the notion o' a sedimentary life. I'm thinkin' o' gaun in for a major; the best yins does it, and ye get a horse.'

In two world wars the proportion of men under arms – both volunteer and conscript – hailing from Clydeside was higher than many other areas of the United Kingdom. The Glasgow area was associated most closely with three infantry regiments: the HLI or Highland Light Infantry, the Royal Scots Fusiliers and the Argyll and Sutherland Highlanders.

On the outbreak of the First World War the territorial as well as the regular battalions were mobilised. In addition, each regiment raised a number of 'service' battalions, which included most famously the 15th or 'Tramways', the 16th or 'Boys Brigade' and the 17th 'Chamber of Commerce', all of the HLI. Best remembered of the military bases was Maryhill Barracks in Glasgow (now the Wyndford housing estate), headquarters for the HLI (and for the Scots Greys cavalry); other substantial depots for infantry in the area included Gailes in

Ayrshire. Other Clydesiders joined the cavalry regiments, the Royal Artillery or the Royal Horse Artillery. Scots regiments were in the thick of the trench warfare, and endured immense casualties, especially at the Somme; more than 500 of the Boys Brigade Battalion died on that battlefield alone. The majority of Scottish units served in France and Flanders, but others were at far-flung Palestine, Salonika and Gallipoli. The 6th Battalion of the Royal Scottish Fusiliers was commanded for a time by the 41-year-old Lieutenant Colonel Winston Spencer Churchill – previously First Lord of the Admiralty but spending some time in the frontline after public criticism of his part in the Gallipoli fiasco of 1915.

The First World War – Mobilisation and the rush to the colours

Britain declared war on Germany on 4 August 1914. Sometime around that date this photograph (**plate 84**), *was taken of a Helensburgh contingent of the newly mobilised Argyll and Sutherland Highlanders Territorial Battalion. The carter and his horse would appear to have been pressed into service to transport a bivouac or similar equipment. In* **plate 85** *the 9th Territorial Battalion of the Argylls is seen performing manoeuvres at Dalinlogart Camp in Argyll in the pre-war years. A disproportionately large number of Scots volunteered to fight at the outbreak of war. A bicycle platoon can be seen on the right flank of the force. A group of older men who served in the Volunteer Force in Lenzie is seen later in the war, in 1916, in* **plate 86**. *Some, though not all, are armed with rifles. They wear Boer War-type hats. In the final plate in this group* (**plate 87**), *we see a recruiting tramcar used by Argyll and Sutherland Highlanders in 1914, complete with bunting and coloured lightbulbs. Posters invite volunteers to 'Fall In'.*

In the short story *Hullo, Glesca Hielanders!* J.J. Bell gives a surprisingly frank description of conditions at the front. Bell's popular character, 'Wee Macgreegor', who is normally occupied with having a good time in Glasgow, joins up with the Glasgow Highlanders and in due course finds himself lying injured in a shell crater, somewhere in France.

Like a trodden, forgotten thing Private Macgregor Robinson lay on the Flanders mud, under the murk and rain. A very long time it seemed since that short, grim struggle amid the blackness and intermittent brightness. The night was still rent with noise and light, but the storm of battle had passed from the place where he had fallen. He could not tell whether his fellows had taken the enemy's trench or retired to their own. He had the vaguest ideas as to where he was. But he knew that there was pain in his left shoulder and right foot, that he was athirst, also that he had killed a man – a big stout man, old enough to have been his father. He tried not to think of the last, though he did not regret it:

it had been a splendid moment. He was not the only soldier lying there
in the mud, but the others, friend or foe, were quite still.

Plate 84

Plate 85 (overleaf)

From a fictional description of the Western Front to an actual account given
by a real private soldier – this extract comes from a letter home by Glasgow man
William Sclater of the 9th HLI, one of only three men from his company to
survive the Somme:

My company had a spell of 48 hours in the firing line . . . the muck is
appalling. Some of our men had simply to be dug out. Our trench was
some 50 hours or so from the enemy's, and we were knee-deep in icy-cold
water. This is a very strange form of warfare . . . We are greatly annoyed
by snipers.

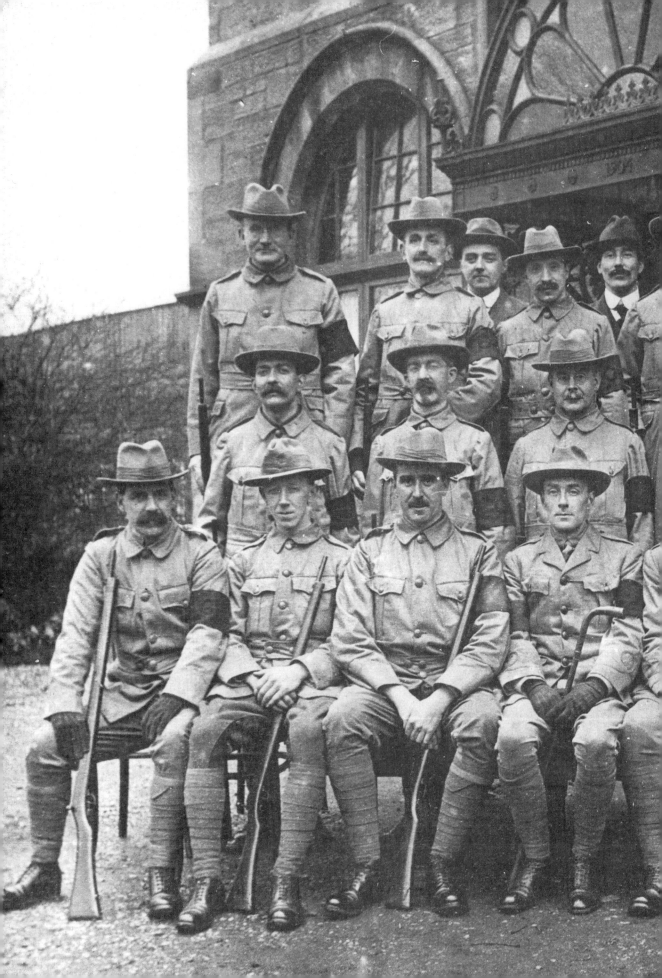

War industry

The demands of the war on the Western Front pointed up the deficiencies in British arms manufacture and a Ministry of Munitions was created under Lloyd George in May 1915 to co-ordinate production. The vast expansion of demand meant that the traditional armaments firms, such as Beardmore's, could no longer cope alone with the demand. Although they continued to make artillery, such as the 8-inch Mark VII howitzer seen in **plate 88**, *war production spread remarkably.*

By the end of the war 22 119 men and 28 087 women were engaged on armaments work in Glasgow and the west of Scotland in factories other than traditional arms manufacturers. From the inception of the Ministry of Munitions to the Armistice these 'new' factories produced, for example, over 8.5 million shells. The stalemate on the Western Front was initially intended to be breached by heavy artillery such as the howitzer, but the tank came to be seen as the war-winning weapon. The tank (the name was originally intended as a codeword but became universally adopted) was first used by the British on the Somme in 1916 but effective use in quantity had to wait until the campaigns of 1918. **Plate 89** *shows a Beardmore-built tank fitted with a 105-horsepower Daimler engine. By the end of the war 90 per cent of all armour plate for British tanks was being produced in the Clyde area and facilities existed there to build 500 tanks a week.*

In the Second World War things were rather different. Fewer territorial and service battalions were required although the Clydeside battalions of the various regiments with a local association were to be found at one time or another in virtually every theatre of war from north-west Europe to Burma.

As well as its contribution to the war effort in men and military units, the Clyde area also had an important role to play in training Allied troops. The local press carried news of foreign units such as the splendidly named Chasseurs d'Alpin billeted near Kirkintilloch, after their evacuation from Norway. While the majority of Scots soldiers under arms were sent to many diverse parts of the globe, a good proportion returned to the west of Scotland as part of the build-up to the invasion of Europe in 1944. The Normandy landings were – some thought – the belated response to demands for a 'Second Front Now', demands which could be seen daubed on walls and pavements in working-class areas like Clydebank. The calls for a Second front to relieve the pressure on the Soviets on the Eastern Front came from 'Uncle Joe' Stalin's many sympathisers on Clydeside, and the street slogans lingered on for years after the war, alongside 'Yanks Go Home'.

In the long build-up for D-Day – probably the greatest turning point of the war – planning for combined operations involving land, sea and air

Plate 88

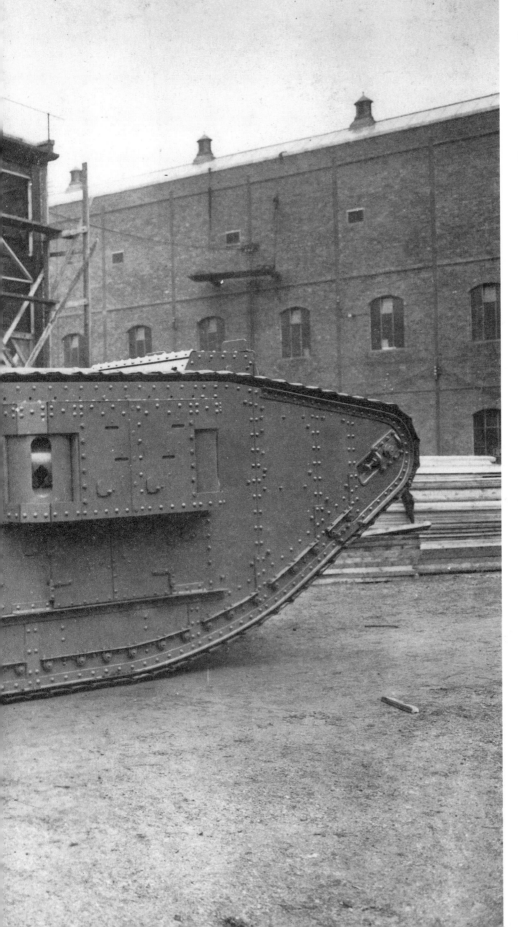

Plate 89

forces was crucial. In June 1940 it was decided to form several commandos, each under one of the Commands within the UK. Locally, numbers 5 and 6 Commando were formed under Western Command, made up of volunteers drawn from the army. Reorganisation took place in October of the same year, and numbers 5 and 6 Commando were absorbed into number 5 Special Service Battalion, which was based at Helensburgh.

West of Scotland beaches were used by British, American and other Allied forces to rehearse landing-craft techniques – this included undercover units such as the Combined Operations Training Centre based at Inveraray on Loch Fyne from 1940. Here commando raids such as the one on the Norwegian Lofoten Islands in March 1941 were planned. On beaches there and in Ayrshire, specialist forces were trained, and techniques developed, which were used during the Torch amphibious landings in North Africa, and the Husky invasion of Sicily. These in turn provided a kind of dress rehearsal for Operation Overlord and the D-Day landings.

The Training Centre at Inveraray for combined operations was formed under Captain J. Hughes-Hallett. By February 1940, no fewer than 5000 officers and ratings had been assigned to the manning of landing craft. As an observer noted, combined operations could put strain on old service loyalties:

> A second Royal Navy was coming into existence, one somewhat disdained by the sea-going Navy who saw it as a sidetrack in their careers, and most were desperate to get back to sea duty. Training was hard and realistic, for it was essential that the landing craft crews got to know their jobs thoroughly before they worked with soldiers on joint exercises, in order that the Army retain its traditional unquestioning faith in the Royal Navy's seamanship. The naval beach parties were selected particularly carefully for theirs was the job of going ashore with the first assault wave and organising the orderly flow of men and stores into the beachhead.

The Second World War – Troops

Following Dunkirk and the fall of France, a number of French troops found their way to the UK, and in this case to the Clydeside town of Kirkintilloch. **Plate 90** *is of a bravely marching contingent, including the band, of the Chasseurs D'Alpin, after their evacuation from the Norway disaster of 1940. In contrast,* **plate 91** *shows Scottish troops whose service has taken them to far-flung battle zones. Men of 216 (Dumbartonshire) Anti-Tank Battery are seen in Egypt in 1944, probably in the Canal Zone. This is some time after the Battle of El Alamein – most of North Africa is in Allied hands and spirits are high. The vehicle is an armoured personnel carrier.*

The loading of British and American troops on to ships for the Torch landings in October 1942 took place both at the Gareloch and upriver at the King George V Dock, which was Glasgow's military embarkation point used by the smaller troopships. They then rendezvoused with the larger transports from Centre Task Force, and the Eastern Task Force from Northern Ireland, in the Outer Firth before beginning their long voyage. The build-up to Torch was the biggest assemblage of troopships and other transports, totalling almost 300 ships, ever seen on the Clyde.

Many Allied forces had first arrived in this country courtesy of countless movements of troopships into the Firth of Clyde, from Canada – the first Canadian troop convoy arrived in the Clyde in December 1939. Five liners carrying 7450 men of the First Canadian Division were escorted by the battle-cruiser *Repulse*, the battleship *Resolution* and the aircraft carrier *Furious*. The ANZAC countries followed suit and, after Pearl Harbor, the troopships came, overwhelmingly, from the USA. It has been calculated that in the course of the war well over a million GIs and other US personnel were shipped to the Tail of the Bank *en route* to bases throughout the UK. The Pride of Clydeside – namely the 'Queens', *Elizabeth* and *Mary* – were responsible, along with other passenger ships, for bringing a substantial proportion of the troops over to these shores. In the United States the GIs had training camps with wooden replicas of the ships on which they practised boarding and stowing their equipment. The very first batch of GIs sailed on the *Queen Mary* from Pier 90 on New York's waterfront in May 1942. Quite symmetrically, at the war's end millions more returned via the Clyde to their homes across the Atlantic. This final massive movement of troops, on a fleet of ships including the 'Queens' once again, was codenamed Operation Magic Carpet.

Plates show evocative images of life on board the *Queen Mary* as she carried many of those American GIs. Winston Churchill recalled in *The Second World War* that Britain had placed the two 'Queens' – the only 80 000-ton ships in the world – at the USA's disposal for this purpose.

> General Marshall asked me how many men we ought to put on board, observing that boats, rafts and other means of flotation could only be provided for about 8000. If this were disregarded they could carry 16 000 men . . . In their first voyages these ships carried only the lesser numbers, but later on they were filled to the brim. As it happened, Fortune stood our friend.

And both of the great liners survived. The log of the *Queen Mary* recorded one such voyage in laconic but graphic fashion:

Plate 90

Plate 91

New York to Gourock, 16 683 souls aboard. New York 25 July 1943. Gourock 30 July 1943. 3353 miles, 4 days, 20 hours, 42 minutes. 28.73 knots. The greatest number of human beings ever embarked on one vessel.

Troopships

The Queen Mary *is seen* (**plate 92**) *at the Tail of the Bank with around 15 000 GIs and other US servicemen in 1944. Both of the 'Queens' and other liners such as the* Normandie *were pressed into service as troopships and used their great speed to elude U-boats — although on one occasion this same speed caused the* Queen Mary *to run down a cruiser escort, the* Curaçao.

Plates taken on board show something of the adaptations that were made to the great liners to accommodate US servicemen. In **plate 93**, *one of the ship's great public rooms has been adapted for American officers, complete with white-jacketed stewards. In contrast, a cabin space* (**plate 94**), *illustrates the way the other ranks were tightly packed on the voyage. The US airmen are playing dice; one of them wears a flying jacket with a pin-up motif and a bomb-tally. Life on board resembled a small town. In this, the year of the Normandy landings, the immense build-up of American forces in Britain was largely made possible by the sailings of the Queens and other great liners.*

The story of the Queens in wartime is one with a truly global dimension. Here is a brief listing showing how the *Queen Mary* ranged across the globe.

When war broke out she was at Pier No. 90 in New York Harbor. From there she made her way to Sydney, where the peacetime fittings were removed, so as to ready her for service as a troopship. On 5 May 1940 she sailed for Greenock with the first load of Australian troops destined for fighting in Europe. Throughout much of 1941 Sydney was her home port and she carried troops for service in the Middle East. When the Japanese moved in the Pacific, she returned to New York and had her troop-carrying capacity increased. US troops were shipped to Australia and then the North Atlantic run began in earnest (along with the *Queen Elizabeth*). Canadian and later US troops were taken across the Atlantic in vast numbers and capacity was increased again. Generally, complete radio silence was observed throughout the crossings and for a large part of the voyage no escort was used. She was equipped with radar from 1942 and a degaussing coil provided some insurance against magnetic mines. On 2 October 1942, in an incident indicative of the immense size and power of these ships, she ran over the cruiser *Curaçao*, which had been provided as an anti-aircraft escort, with the loss of all hands, while both vessels were zig-zagging at a speed of 28.5 knots. In 1945 she was part of a great fleet which sailed from the Clyde with thousands of homeward-bound troops. During the six years of war the Prime Minister and other VIPs often travelled on the RMS *Queen Mary* – another immensely dramatic episode involving the River Clyde in wartime.

As already indicated, Clydeside was deeply involved in the movement and equipping the armada of seaborne forces assembled for the Normandy landings. Large sections of the ingenious 'Mulberry Harbours' – a key part of the master plan for invasion – were assembled in Lanarkshire. The same J. Hughes-Hallett (now Commodore) who had commanded at Inveraray, was credited with the original idea of a 'Mulberry Harbour', which Churchill in his history of the war described as:

> A large area of sheltered water protected by a breakwater based on blockships brought to the scene by their own power and then sunk in a prearranged position.

The concept was established, but became increasingly sophisticated:

> The whole project was majestic. On the beaches themselves would be the great piers, with their seaward ends afloat and sheltered. At these piers coasters and landing-craft would be able to discharge at all states of the tide. To protect them against the wanton winds and waves break-waters would be spread in a great arc to seaward, enclosing a large area of sheltered water.

Plate 92 (overleaf)

Plate 93

When June 1944 arrived, these fabricated artificial harbours did indeed provide shelter for the huge fleet of support vessels bringing men and supplies across the Channel, until Allied forces could break out from the beaches. As mentioned in another chapter, the weel-kent Clyde paddle steamer *Talisman* was one of many Clyde-built ships there in the English Channel and she saw service as a headquarters ship for the Mulberry Harbours. And, as already indicated, there was another connection with the west of Scotland. The *Motherwell Times* of 11 April 1945 reported:

> Warm congratulations to Lanarkshire workers . . . were extended by Rear Admiral H. Hickling, CBE, DSO, who had charge of the construction of the harbour on the Normandy beaches, when he paid a visit to Messrs Alex. Findlay & Co's Parkneuk Works at Motherwell . . . The whole success of the invasion depended on the 'Mulberry' and without it they could have had no guarantee that the vital supplies for

our armed forces could have been landed. Of the 23 pierheads in the
Mulberry, 18 were constructed by this firm.

Plate 94

Yet again, the workers of Clydeside had put together one of the crucial
building blocks of Allied victory.

CHAPTER 5

The home front

Keep the home-fires burning,
Though your heart is yearning,
Though the boys are far away,
We dream of you.

Popular song

Plate 95
*Two women mechanics at
Prestwick working on an
Avro Lancaster bomber.*

'The home front' was a phrase coined in imitation of military usage, but it represents the impact of war on the daily life of its civilian population. If not in the First World War, certainly in the second, there was a real possibility of invasion, most likely in the south of England. Despite this, institutions such as the Citizen Training Force of 1914 and the Second World War Local Defence Volunteers (or Home Guard), Auxiliary Fire Services, Observer Corps, Special Constables and other units of civil defence such as the Air Raid Precautions (ARP) were enthusiastically supported throughout the whole of the UK.

The Lennox in the First World War

As the Germans advanced through Belgium and into France, some refugees from 'gallant little Belgium' made their way to Britain. Seen here in **plate 96** *is a mixed-age group of Belgian refugees who found a billet in the Dumbartonshire village of Lenzie. Also at Lenzie a number of wounded servicemen (* **plate 97** *) are being entertained by the locals. The probability is that these are officers, because of the visibly middle-class status of the hosts (a committee no doubt). Finally, a group of elderly Lennoxtown Special Constables appear in* **plate 98***.*

These various forms of what might be called a people's militia reflected a readiness for coping with invasion even though such a thing had not occurred for hundreds of years. One of Winston Churchill's Prime Ministerial directives ran:

> If this island is seriously invaded everyone in it will immediately receive orders either to 'Carry on' or to 'Stand firm'. In the vast majority of cases the order will be to 'Carry on' . . . the order 'Stand firm' applies only to those districts where fighting is actually going on, and is

BELGIAN REFUGEES IN LENZIE.

Plate 96

intended to make sure that there will be no fugitives blocking the roads, and that everyone who has decided to stay in a likely area of attack will stand firm in his dwelling or centre till the enemy in the neighbourhood have been destroyed or driven out.

In 1939 the *Hamilton Advertiser* printed a report illustrating the way that these ideas came down to a local level:

A parade comprising a detachment of the 6th Battalion Cameronians (Scottish Rifles) . . . headed by a pipe band, with six motor transport trucks in the rear, marched from Muirhall to the Regal Picture House on Thursday evening to see *The Warning*, a film portraying what might happen in the event of an actual raid on this country. *The Warning*, with its grimly realistic picture of what might happen should Britain be invaded from the air, and displaying impressively the organisation of a city to cope with explosions, gas and fire, ended with a call to national service spoken by Sir John Anderson.

Plate 97

Anderson was the government minister in charge of civil defence, who lent his name to the corrugated iron air-raid shelter – the Anderson Shelter – to be found in many back gardens. Other forms of shelter were being installed – many wartime reminiscences mention the danger of colliding in the blackout with a baffle-wall built to minimise bomb blast at a tenement-close mouth. On the actual eve of the declaration of war (2 September 1939) the *Glasgow Evening News* reported that Glasgow's organisation for defence against air attack 'has now been completed'. Safeguarding tenements with steel struts and reinforcing closes was:

> being tackled vigorously; trenches are being dug in the public parks and police officers are patrolling the streets, carrying their steel helmets and gas masks . . . [By November] another underground shelter with accommodation for 700 persons is to be constructed off the Gallowgate in the railway tunnel under the site of the old barracks.

Plate 98

Plate 99

Women at war – First World War

A group of plates follow in which we see women engaged in war work of one kind or another. It is well known that the active participation of many women in vital tasks during the 1914–18 war was an important factor in their gaining the vote when hostilities ceased. **Plate 99** *shows a group of women in Kirkintilloch rolling bandages for use at the front. They are under the supervision of medical staff, and, interestingly, the hats are probably being worn to prevent some contamination of the bandages. Next, in* **plate 100**, *is a female Glasgow street lamplighter, one of eighty women employed in this way in 1915. In this case women took over what was previously regarded as man's work. They earned between 17 and 28 shillings a week and worked for fifty-one hours. The plate is from a file in the Imperial War Museum called 'Women's War Work – Corporation of Glasgow'. Another First World War example of wartime women workers is this portrait (***plate 101***) of two young women employed at the Southbank Iron Works, Kirkintilloch. Note the complete unsuitability of the footwear for such heavy and dirty work.*

To turn to the actual nature of domestic involvement in the two global wars
of the last century, the direct impact of war and death-dealing weapons on
the Clyde came not from an invasion of foreign troops, but, as we have seen,
from the arial attacks launched by the Luftwaffe in the Second World War. The
nature of people's experience then was very different from what they had had
in the First World War. In the latter, mass popular enthusiasm was reflected,
for example, in the 'rush to the colours' at the war's outset, promoted by a
wide range of recruiting stunts like 'recruiting tramcars'. At the same time,
well-known manifestations of war Hysteria (the showing of ' white feathers'
and so on), were less apparent in the Clyde area than elsewhere; indeed

there was a certain amount of left-wing militancy to which the government responded by coining the term 'Red Clydeside' and jailing some of the men's leaders.

Second World War volunteers

*Taken in 1940, **plate 102** shows the Dumbarton Home Guard relaxing after exercises in the hills behind the town. Very near to this point was constructed one of the 'dummy towns' as popular descriptions had it – the series of lights and flares codenamed Starfish, erected in the hills on both banks of the Clyde to act as a decoy to enemy bombing missions. The dominant thought in defence planners' minds in the later 1930s was that 'the bomber would always get through'. The experience of the bombing of Guernica (April 1937) by the German Condor Legion during the Spanish Civil War reinforced this concept and there was serious concern that high-explosive, incendiary and gas attacks from the air would present an entirely new scale of threat to society. As part of the package of Air Raid Precautions (ARP) measures taken by the British Government from 1935 onwards an Auxiliary Fire Service was formed in 1938 to create a body of trained volunteer fire-fighters to work alongside the regular fire service personnel in coping with the bombing threat. The AFS was mobilised on 1 September 1939 and control of fire services was transferred from local authorities to central government with the creation of the National Fire Service in 1941. **Plate 103** shows a group of Greenock firemen, of mixed ranks, enjoying a cup of tea from a mobile canteen presented to the town by the Order of the Eastern Star in Canada; the fireman on the left is wearing a helmet with the Auxiliary Fire Service logo. Much of the damage done by the Greenock blitz and other aerial attacks was due to the mixture of high-explosive and incendiary devices that was used. The high-explosive bombs knocked down buildings and killed people but also damaged essential infrastructure such as water mains and power supplies. The incendiary bombs could then do their work of burning down the damaged towns, and fires would be more difficult to control because of the problems of interrupted water supply and fractured gas mains. In the attack on Clydeside on 13/14 March 1941 (the first night of the Clydebank blitz) 236 German aircraft dropped 272 tons of high explosive and 1650 incendiary canisters. **Plate 104** shows a Greenock fireman demonstrating how to deal with an incendiary.*

Plate 101

In the Second World War, there was a growing awareness of the need to shelve political differences during the emergency. The remarkable fact is that a government, led by arch-Tory Winston Churchill (who was never entirely trusted by some workers), did manage to 'co-exist' in Scotland with a reforming Labour Secretary of State. The latter was Clydesider Tom Johnston (who had been rather less of an Establishment figure in the First World War when he had edited a determinedly anti-war Scottish weekly called *Forward*).

Gift to the people of
GREENOCK
from the
ER OF THE EASTERN STA
(DISTRICTS 10, 11 & 19)
CANADA
commemoration of the late
QUEEN VICTORIA

Plate 102 (previous page)

Plate 103

Plate 104

Faces of Clydeside

Some visitors to the Clyde were show-biz celebrities such as Bob Hope who came to entertain the troops and other servicemen. Here in **plate 105**, *an audience of Denny shipyard workers are being entertained in their dinner hour by a band of the Royal Marines. The yard's rails can be seen underfoot, while more workers watch from their perches in the stocks in the background. One young worker is still wearing her Dumbarton Academy school scarf.*

*This cartoon (***plate 106***) is an amusing Scottish Field illustration of a Glasgow tea-room in wartime. Taken from a series of sketches called 'The Home Front', it depicts something of the cosmopolitan air of Glasgow when its tea-rooms and other places of rest and recreation were crammed with visiting servicemen – Canadians, Poles Australians and Free French among them. And this appeared in December 1941, even before the Yanks arrived!*

From 1939 onwards, it is probably fair to say that there was a dogged acceptance of the impact of total war on everyday life in Scotland, and this remained the case throughout the six-year duration. Following the Clydebank blitz, men who had been on strike at John Brown's, the yard which built the great Cunarders, went back to work immediately.

What is largely forgotten now is that there was some resentment at the fact that shipyard and engineering workers were in reserved occupations and were at the same time earning good money from working 'plenty of overtime': *The Lennox Herald*, a Dumbarton newspaper, had described the background in late September of 1939:

Plate 105 (overleaf)

> Workers in the Clyde shipyards and engineering establishments have received permission to work all overtime required . . . following a conference between the Confederation of Shipbuilding and Engineering Unions (Clyde District Committee), the Clyde Shipbuilders Association and the North-West Engineering Trades Employers Association.

Typical of the west of Scotland mentality, however, some degree of scepticism remained and there was a pretty high proportion of conscientious objectors in the area, some of whom volunteered for highly dangerous war work such the bomb-disposal squads.

The impact of total war from 1939 until 1945 was all-pervasive – it could be found in everything from the visible impact of civil defence, rationing and austerity to the more insidious effects of propaganda, security and censorship. 'Germany calling' was the well-known wartime preamble to the regular broadcasts from Germany of William Joyce, the propagandist who was universally known as 'Lord Haw-Haw' to his derisive listeners in this country. This war propaganda was sometimes clever, more rarely effective, but no one with memories of these times will forget by what a large margin that sort of thing missed its mark. He drew a response of jibes and frank disbelief – nowhere more than Clydeside, though Goebbels had specially 'targeted' Scotland with his 'Scottish Transmitter'. That was based on the rather dubious premise that anti-English feeling in Scotland could be played upon and form the basis of a national uprising. In a graphic and only lightly fictionalised account of these days called *In His Fashion*, J. Harris Saunders, a principal teacher who was warden or leader at the Vale of Leven Academy Rest Centre, wrote:

> This feeling of being in it was sustained by the persistent rumour that the unspeakable 'Lord Haw-Haw' had promised the [Alexandria] Torpedo Factory a Luftwaffe visit that would crumble its great marble staircase.

Plate 106

On the other hand 'the wireless' – in the shape of the BBC – did have a profoundly important influence on national morale and patriotism, and contributed to Angus Calder's notion of 'The People's War'. The wartime Head of BBC Listener Research stressed the immense importance of radio. He picked out the BBC's news bulletins as absolutely crucial elements of national life:

> The news bulletins invariably stood out as peaks in the daily listening curve: the largest were at six and nine p.m., when on a typical day their audiences would be anything from 30 to 50 per cent of the population.

On special occasions, as when it was known that the Prime Minister would speak, the listening audiences would be even greater – usually over 60 per cent. On the evening of D-Day, by which time it was known that the Allied Armies had at last landed in Normandy, 80 per cent listened at nine p.m.

Newspapers and magazines were more traditional channels of information which occasionally highlighted significant wartime social change, such as women's war work. Articles and features followed land-girls working on farms throughout the country and recorded the work done by women in munitions factories. Mostly though, they preferred to build morale with articles about wartime fashion – typically about 'how to help with the war effort and stay beautiful at the same time'.

Plate 107 (overleaf)

Women in the Second World War

Plate 107 *is of Mrs Agnes Smith, a forewoman in charge of a squad of forty-five women working in Scott's shipyard in Greenock in June 1942. This mother of ten had personal experience of most of the trades required in the shipyard; she had also worked in an engineering shop in the First World War. Her husband worked in another Clyde yard.*

In **plate 108**, *a young member of Scott's women's squad – Mary Cunningham – is seen on her first solo job as an apprentice welder. She is holding a welder's helmet aloft. A merchant ship can be seen in the background. A Wren (member of the Women's Royal Naval Service) dispatch rider is delivering a message to a petty officer from the corvette convoy escort tied up behind him, in* **plate 109**. *Note that the motorcycle has a hooded headlamp because of blackout regulations.*

In lighter mood, **plate 110** *shows a Chief Officer Nye of the WRNS, appearing as the Good Fairy in a production of the pantomime Cinderella before an audience of uniformed colleagues. They are at their base in a requisitioned Greenock house.*

The feeling of day-to-day life on Clydeside in wartime can be conjured up from reflective pieces in newspapers such as the Glasgow dailies and evening papers, and from various memoirs (like Saunders' account) which looked back at these years.

During the First World War the novelist Neil Munro's columns in the *Glasgow Evening News*, under the byline 'The Looker-on', gave glimpses of people's lives and work in the villages and towns of the west coast, as well as in the city of Glasgow. In 'The Looker-on', Munro's immensely popular characters of Para Handy and Erchie MacPherson (both Clydesiders of course) gave a humorous boost to morale (as did J.J. Bell's Wee Macgreegor in the *Evening Times*), without ever appearing as a mouthpiece of government propaganda – no small feat when propaganda could be very heavy-handed indeed.

Something of the confused feeling of the first year and a half of the Second World War, right up to the rude awakening of the Clydebank blitz, can be gained by these further extracts from *In His Fashion*, which give a distinctively Scottish slant to what is as much memoir as novel:

Never was the British nation's survival hope more shaky than in that autumn of 1940. It stood alone, thrown on its own meagre material resources, mostly brought in by unsung merchant seamen through submarine-ridden seas . . . The arrival of more and more Canadian volunteers heartened all who had any contact with these cheerful young men longing for a 'bash at the Hun' . . . The blackout lay heavy on civilian morale. Workers left home in pitch-darkness for factories now seriously tackling the problem of war production, and returned home in pitch-darkness . . . As things turned out, Nemesis was just around the

corner, or rather up there in the sky. It was not written that Goering should spare the Clydeside, or his pilots be unable to find it through its habitual mantle of fog and industrial smut . . .

Saunders gives us this description of the aftermath of the bombing as refugees from Clydebank began to arrive at reception centres, such as his Vale of Leven Academy Rest Centre:

As more and more buses kept arriving the scene became more and more tragic and chaotic. And still they came – the old, the middle-aged, the young, frail old men and women, buxom and blousy hussies, goggle-eyed,

Plate 110

bare-legged flappers, night shift workmen still in their dungarees, dishevelled mothers with puling infants in their arms, wee laddies clutching caged canaries or budgies or leading mongrels on a string, the 'walking wounded' with grimy bloodstained bandages, most of them laden with paper parcels, cardboard boxes, battered attaché cases, containing the little they had been able to save and remove of their worldly possessions.

By the time of the second great conflict the art of photographic journalism, in newspapers such as *The Bulletin* and magazines like *Scottish Field*, had so advanced as to provide other kinds of lasting image of what was termed the home front. If this was about the realistic face of war, opportunities for 'escapism' were just as important to wartime morale. The people of Clydeside, for instance, continued their long-standing love affair with the moving picture throughout the period. Dr MacPhail's *The Clydebank Blitz* described the films on offer at the five local cinemas or 'picture houses' on the evening of the first bombing raids in March 1941:

Shirley Temple and Jack Oakie could be seen in *Young People* at the La Scala and the Regal, Dalmuir. Jean Hersholt, starred as the 'pocket

Plate 111

Ginger Rogers', was on view at the Pavilion; at the Bank Cinema there was a film about horse-racing in America called *Maryland* and at the Palace, in addition to the film, *Daughter of the Tong*, Carrol Levis was on show with his 'Discoveries' [a talent show]. Many people were to spend the first hours of the blitz in these cinemas. It was the normal procedure when an air raid alert was sounded for the manager to inform the audience, some of whom of necessity had to leave, while the majority usually remained in their seats; and as there had been no raid in Clydebank since before the New Year, most people on March 13 tended to stay put at first. When it became evident, however that bombs were dropping all over Clydebank, the programmes came to an end but many stayed on in the cinemas, gathering under the balcony for safety.

Plate 112 (opposite)

Visitors to the Clyde

War brought many distinguished visitors to Clydeside. **Plate 111** *shows General Charles de Gaulle (left) and Admiral Philippe Auboyneau, Commander-in-Chief of the Free French Navy (right) in Greenock on 24 December 1942, with an unidentified French lieutenant de vaisseau. Before visiting the Free French naval base at Greenock, de Gaulle, the leader of the Free French Government in exile, had visited a hospital for French sailors established on the other shore of the Clyde at Knockderry Castle, Cove.*

King Haakon VII of Norway went into exile in Britain in June 1940 after the German invasion of his country. He is pictured in **plate 112** *at Glasgow on 21 December 1941 for the launch of a 7073-ton cargo vessel built for the Norwegian Government at the Whiteinch yard of Barclay, Curle and Company. The ship, named* King Haakon VII, *was launched by Mrs Sunde (pictured with the king), the wife of the Minister of Supply in the Norwegian Government in exile. On a later visit to the Clyde (October 1944) the king was, in a delightful piece of historical humour, made a Freeman of the Burgh of Largs – the place where his namesake Haakon IV had been defeated by the Scots in 1263, a defeat which brought about the end of Norse power in Scotland. (A current enemy who visited the Clyde was Rudolf Hess.)*

One of the many visits to the Clyde in wartime by King George VI and Queen Elizabeth is depicted in **plate 113**. *The royal couple have arrived at Greenock on board the TSMV* Ashton, *which had been built by William Denny and Brothers of Dumbarton for service between central Glasgow and the 1938 Empire Exhibition site at Bellahouston. On the outbreak of war she was requisitioned as a tender. On a later occasion, the king is visiting the Clyde and the battleship* King George V. *As the royal party are piped aboard we see in* **plate 114** *the queen being welcomed by the ship's captain. A young Princess Elizabeth stands at the ship's rail.*

In **plate 115** *Prime Minister Winston Churchill disembarks from* Queen Mary *in 1943, after the voyage from Clyde across the Atlantic to Halifax for the Quebec Conference with President Roosevelt. Stokers and other servicemen are seen at the open door. An armed US sailor stands guard.*

Plate 113

Plate 114

Among the cinema audiences would be servicemen and women on leave in their home town, and others who were engaged in what was later called 'rest and recreation'. The hotels, cinemas and dance halls of Glasgow, in particular, were a magnet for Allied servicemen from all over the world – Evelyn Waugh gives a bleak but evocative description of the city as it was in late 1940 in his novel, *Officers and Gentlemen*. Trimmer, a character who is 'attached' to a commando unit on the fictitious island of Mugg, manages to wangle some leave and goes looking for 'the lights' in Glasgow:

> Glasgow in November 1940 was not literally a *ville lumiere*. Fog and crowds gave the black-out a peculiar density. Trimmer, on the afternoon of his arrival, went straight from the train to the station hotel. Here too were fog and crowds. All its lofty halls and corridors were heaped with

luggage and thronged by transitory soldiers and sailors . . .

Full, Dickensian fog enveloped the city. Day and night the streets
were full of slow-moving, lighted trams and lorries and hustling
coughing people. Sea-gulls emerged and suddenly vanished overhead.
The rattle and the shuffle and the hooting of motor-horns drowned the
warnings of distant ships. Now and then the air-raid sirens rose above
all. The hotel was always crowded. Between drinking hours soldiers and
sailors slept in the lounges. When the bars opened they awoke to call
plaintively for a drink.

Plate 115 (overleaf)

Waugh, who drew on his own experience for *Officers and Gentlemen*, doesn't tell
us the name of the station hotel, but we do know that Naval HQ Glasgow was
established in St Enoch's Hotel.

Women at war is a theme which emerges in many of the photographs taken
during the two world wars; they are seen doing the jobs of tram guards and
lamplighters, and in ironworks and shipyards, as well as in the voluntary organi-
sations and the uniformed services. Most women had more conventional roles,
and enduring was certainly one of them. Twice in thirty years the people of
Clydeside had to try and come to terms with rationing and austerity, with inter-
minable queues and searching out of precious items such as coal. Neil Munro
describes this in a First World War story called 'Duffy in the Dark'. In this
Erchie Macpherson's friend Duffy the coal merchant is driving his lorry home,
'whistling the war-song of the trade – "Keep the Home-fires Burning"'. On the
other hand, less cheery attitudes to austerity and the sheer bone weariness of
civilians after a long war comes through in another Erchie story, 'Celebrating
Peace'. When asked why he isn't out celebrating the signing of the Peace Treaty
at Versailles in June 1919, Erchie makes his feelings clear in a heartfelt speech
which could be seen as a suitable epilogue to the whole experience of war in the
twentieth century:

'I'm no' gaun to cheer till the last British sodger's landed on this side o'
the English Channel and back at his tred; till the Territorials is gaun to
camp at Stobs or Gailes at the Fair wi' red coats on and a toppin' brass
band for their gymkana; till butter and beef's demobilised.'

'And beer,' suggested Duffy.

'Till the Gleska tramcar system is equal to its reputation, till the
factors are chasin' folk up to rent their hooses; till a trip doon the watter
wi' high tea included is again within the means o' a waiter; till oranges
are a ha'penny, bananas a penny, eggs a shillin' a dozen, and the kipper
herring again in the home o' the British workin' man.'

Following the second great conflict of the twentieth century, there was
something of the same resignation and humour to be found. The *Kirkintilloch
Herald* announced on 19 December 1945:

Plate 116 (previous page)

> The Home Guard is to be disbanded on December 31, 1945, when
> members will cease to be liable to recall and the uniform which they
> have been authorised to retain will become their personal property, the
> War Office announces. A district man who has continued to give the
> Home Guard as his excuse for going out on certain evenings of the week
> will not welcome the publication of the above.

The Clyde full circle

*An important arm of the aircraft-building industry in the 1939–45 war was the Blackburn factory
in Dumbarton. Probably the best-known plane built there was the Short S-25 General Reconnaissance
Sunderland flying-boat which was used extensively by Coastal Command in the war against the U-
boat. The Sunderland was a huge aircraft (85 feet long with a wingspan of 112 feet), with four
Pegasus engines and a two-deck structure, carrying a large crew and even boasting a separate officers'
wardroom. Armament comprised machine-guns in a rotating nose turret and tail turret. There was
also a dorsal turret in some models and bombs and depth-charges were carried on racks in the fuselage.*
Plate 116 *shows a Mark III Sunderland landing on the River Clyde at Dumbarton Rock, with the
Blackburn factory out of sight behind the Rock. Four high-explosive bombs fell on Dumbarton Rock
in May 1941, the first time it had been attacked by an enemy in three centuries.*

*This striking image provides a suitable conclusion to the visual story of the Clyde at war, in
which* Alcluith, *the earliest important strategic feature of the river, forms a backdrop to a
twentieth-century aircraft used in global warfare.*

INDEX